FOREWORD

The interests of justice and the interests of the child are not alternatives. Children have a right to justice and their evidence is essential if society is to protect their interests and deal effectively with those who would harm them.

All too often the interests of justice have been frustrated - and the child further harmed by the legal process - because it has just not been possible for the child to cope with a full court appearance, or for the court to take proper account of what he or she has to say.

In 1988 the Government acted to allow child witnesses to give evidence from outside the courtroom via a special television link, and to ease the rules about child witnesses. This programme of reform was continued and extended in the Criminal Justice Act 1991. For the first time video recordings of earlier interviews with police and social workers can be played to the court as part of the trial.

This is a major step forward. Together with the other reforms made by and alongside the 1991 Act it represents a great improvement for child witnesses. We owe it to them to make the best possible use of the new procedures.

Our two Departments have worked closely together to develop this Memorandum of Good Practice. They were greatly assisted in the task by a special steering group. This included professionals from different disciplines and the voluntary sector, working together to test and further develop the guidance. By working in close harmony with your colleagues, you the practitioner will be able to make the guidance work for children and for justice.

MICHAEL JACK
Home Office

TIM YEO
Department of Health

CONTENTS

HOME OFFICE *in conjunction with* DEPARTMENT OF HEALTH

[signature]

MEMORANDUM OF GOOD PRACTICE

ON VIDEO RECORDED INTERVIEWS WITH CHILD WITNESSES FOR CRIMINAL PROCEEDINGS

LONDON: HMSO

Designed by Home Office Design and Illustration Branch

MEMBERS OF THE POLICY STEERING GROUP

Mr Alan Cogbill, Home Office, **Chair** *(until December 1991)*
Miss Christine Stewart, Home Office, **Chair** *(from January 1992)*

Mr Jim Aldridge, Police Scientific Development Branch
Mrs Rosemary Arkley, Social Services Inspectorate
Professor Diane Birch, Department of Law, Nottingham University
Professor Ray Bull, Department of Psychology,
   Portsmouth Polytechnic
Mr Tony Butler, Association of Chief Police Officers
Professor Graham Davies, British Psychological Society
Mr Mark de Pulford, Home Office Criminal Policy Department
Mr Jim Dickinson, HM Inspectorate of Constabulary
   (until February 1992)
Mr Roger Ede, The Law Society
Mr Mike Gardiner, Association of County Councils
Mrs Moira Gibb, Association of Directors of Social Services
Chief Superintendant Ian Herd, Home Office Police Department
Miss Valerie Howarth, ChildLine
Dr David Jones, Royal College of Psychiatrists
Dr Steve Lewis, Police Scientific Development Branch
Ms Joyce Moseley, Association of Metropolitan Authorities
Ms Maureen O'Hara, Children's Legal Centre
Ms Angela Palmer, Crown Prosecution Service
Mr David Purkiss, HM Inspectorate of Constabulary
   (from March 1992)
Mr Peter Smith, National Children's Bureau
Commander David Stevens, Metropolitan Police
Miss Kathleen Taylor, Department of Health
Ms Jane Tunstill,
   National Council of Voluntary Child Care Organisations
Dr Eileen Vizard, The Tavistock Clinic
Ms Corinne Wattam, NSPCC
Miss Adele Williams, Criminal Bar Association
Mr Paul Zimmermann, Lord Chancellor's Department

Ms Sue Jago, Home Office, **Secretary**

INTRODUCTION

Good practice in making videos of child interviews should help the child and justice

The main purpose of this Memorandum is to help those making a video recording of an interview with a child witness *where it is intended that the result should be acceptable in criminal proceedings.* Such a recording can spare the child from having to recount *evidence*[1] to the court in person and provide a highly valuable, early record of the child's account. If handled properly, the video recorded interview will be in the interests of the child and in the interests of justice.

The Home Office consulted widely in drawing up this Memorandum

The Memorandum draws upon the recommendations of the Home Office Advisory Group on Video Evidence, chaired by His Honour Judge Thomas Pigot QC, and its preparation included a wide-ranging consultation exercise between the relevant Government departments and professionals with practical experience of the different aspects of the investigation of child abuse. The membership of the steering group which oversaw the development of this Memorandum is set out on the page facing this Introduction. The guidance in the Memorandum is, however, the responsibility of the Home Office in conjunction with the Department of Health.

The Memorandum relates to criminal proceedings

The focus of the Memorandum is necessarily on criminal proceedings. It does not provide a guide to everything that needs to be known by those making video recordings of children, nor can it be fully comprehensive about criminal proceedings. It should not, therefore, be used in isolation but rather as a resource to be added to knowledge gained from training and the practitioner's own expertise. The guidance in the Memorandum is not a universal prescription: each child is unique and the effective interview will be one which is tailored to the child's particular needs and circumstances.

The guidance in the Memorandum is voluntary

A video recording that does not strictly comply with the Memorandum will not automatically be ruled inadmissible. On the contrary, it was Parliament's clear intention that such video recordings of children's testimony should be admitted unless, in the opinion of the judge, it would clearly be contrary to the interests of justice to do so. The Memorandum is therefore voluntary but should be followed whenever practicable to try to ensure that a video recording will be acceptable in a criminal court.

Working Together

The Memorandum builds on the 'Working Together' approach

The 1987 report by Lord Justice Butler-Sloss on child abuse in Cleveland[2] made a number of recommendations about the investigation of alleged offences against children and the conduct of interviews. The Report recognised that, since the early 1970s, the key to effective action was a close working relationship between the professional agencies involved. This multi-agency approach and the Butler-Sloss guidance on interviewing children, was explained in the joint Government departments' inter-agency guide 'Working Together'[3] and affirmed in circulars and guidance from the Home

---

[1]Evidence in chief, see annex A.
[2]Report of the Inquiry into Child Abuse 1987.
[3]HMSO 1988; revised edition 1991.

1

Office, Department of Health, Department of Education and Science and the Welsh Office. The guidance in this Memorandum builds explicitly on the Butler-Sloss and 'Working Together' approach and is compatible with it. It does not affect the need to take full account of all the circumstances of the case and the views of other agencies before deciding that criminal proceedings will be appropriate.

Working Together teams need to respond to the recent changes in the law addressed by this Memorandum

A major element in the 'Working Together' approach is joint interviewing by police and social workers. This will only be effective where police officers and social workers have appropriate training and are regularly employed in joint agency childcare investigations. The formation of specialist teams, adequately trained, within the respective agencies, will foster best practice. Many areas already have facilities for video recording interviews with children who are suspected victims of abuse. Some of the ground covered by this Memorandum will be familiar to those involved in joint investigations. However, the reforms to the law about child evidence and procedure made by the Criminal Justice Act 1991 introduce a new set of considerations and challenges for 'Working Together' teams. *Practitioners will need to prepare carefully in order to make the best of the reforms, both in the interests of the child and of justice.*

Video recordings and the Criminal Justice Act 1991

Understanding how video recordings may be used in court under the changes made by the Criminal Justice Act 1991 requires some familiarity with the basic procedures and terms used in a criminal trial. A glossary of terms appears at annex A.

The Criminal Justice Act 1991 says a video can replace a child's evidence in a criminal court

A *video recording*[4] of an interview with a child may be admissible in the *Crown Court*[4] or a *youth court*[4] (but not *magistrates' courts*[4]). In the case of youth courts, if no video equipment is available, proceedings may be held in a suitably equipped Crown Court Centre. Under the provisions made by the Criminal Justice Act 1991, *the child*[4] will not be allowed to be *examined in chief*[4] on any matter which, in the opinion of the court, has been dealt with in his or her recorded testimony. *Provided, then, that the recorded interview covers the matters which would otherwise be dealt with in chief, the recording takes the place of the first stage of the child's evidence.* That is the end of the function of the recording: *cross-examination*[4] and re-examination, if proceedings get that far, are conducted by questioning the child 'live' at the trial. But the 1991 Act continues its protection of the child by barring the accused from cross-examining in person and by ensuring that *live television link*[4] apparatus can be used so that the child is seen and heard in court on television monitors without ever having to appear in the court room. The use of such apparatus is at the discretion of the judge but permission is granted in almost all cases.

The use of a video recording for evidential purposes in this way is new and quite exceptional. *The questioning by the police officer or social worker, in effect, replaces examination of the child by an advocate in open court.*

But the court can reject or edit the video if it is not in the interests of justice

Therefore, video interviewers will need to understand the basic rules of evidence

The Criminal Justice Act 1991 gives the court power to reject the video recording, or any part of it, on the grounds that "in the *interests of justice*"[4] it ought not to be admitted. Since a key reason for making the recording is to spare the child, as far as possible, from giving his or her evidence at the trial, the interviewer must be aware of the circumstances in which a court may decide that it is not in the interests of justice to admit all or part of the recording. It is here that joint investigating teams will need to develop a clear appreciation of the

---

[4]See annex A.

framework of the rules of evidence in criminal cases. Their members are *not* expected to mimic advocates, but they will need to take proper account of the rules and the law in interviewing children.

Training

Members of 'Working Together' teams should be trained and should be familiar with this Memorandum

The Butler-Sloss Report recommended that all interviews should be undertaken only by those with training, experience and an aptitude for talking to children. That recommendation was fully endorsed by those involved in preparing this Memorandum, with the additional recommendation that, save in wholly exceptional circumstances, no-one should undertake any interview with a child witness which is to be video recorded for the purposes of criminal proceedings unless he or she is properly conversant with this Memorandum. Those who are responsible for convening joint investigating teams will need to review practice and see to it that the various professional skills and specialised expertise necessary to make a successful video recording are satisfactorily represented amongst team members. Training programmes capable of delivering and maintaining those skills should be in place and regularly reviewed in the light of practice development. Every opportunity should be taken to promote mutual inter-agency understanding on a professional and personal level. That will be enhanced by joint training.

Video recordings made by the defence

The defence can also submit video recordings for evidential purposes and Part 1 of the Memorandum is particularly relevant to them

This Memorandum is written on the assumption that the video recording is being prepared for use as part of the prosecution case. Except where the contrary is indicated, the legal position is the same as regards recordings made for inclusion as defence evidence. Video recordings by the defence are not expected to be as common as those made for prosecution purposes (see also Part 2, paragraph 2.29 for guidance on seeking consent). However, much of the advice, and particularly that in Part 1 of this Memorandum, is also appropriate for anyone considering preparing video recordings for the defence and it is strongly recommended for that purpose.

Interview objectives

These are not therapeutic interviews

It is very important that those conducting interviews under this Memorandum have clear, agreed objectives which are consistent with the main purpose, which is to listen with an open mind to what the child has to say, if anything, about the alleged event. The interviews described in this Memorandum are not and should never be referred to as "therapeutic interviews". Nor should the term "disclosure interview" ever be used to describe them. Although it may well be that the child does confirm details of what is suspected by others, and that the interview may serve a therapeutic or other objective, therapy is not the primary aim of these interviews.

Civil proceedings

Video recordings may also be admissible in civil proceedings

One important reason for video recording interviews with children is to reduce the number of times that they are called upon to repeat their accounts during the investigation of the case. As noted earlier, this Memorandum concentrates on the evidential implications for criminal proceedings. At the time the interview is planned, it may not be known whether criminal proceedings will follow and, even if it is, civil proceedings concerned with the welfare of the child, and which would also benefit from a video recorded interview, may well come first. In such circumstances the interview might need to serve objectives[5] which are additional to, and no less important than, those with which this Memorandum is primarily concerned. There is no reason why such objectives cannot be met within a single interview, provided it is properly prepared. The rules of evidence which apply to *civil proceedings*[4] are generally less stringent, and so is the *burden of proof*[4]. From those perspectives a video recording prepared according to the standards recommended in this Memorandum is likely to be suitable for civil cases. However, it may not be necessary or even appropriate to adopt the Memorandum's event- oriented approach when *only* particular civil proceedings, for example matrimonial proceedings, are contemplated.

Contents of the Memorandum

Organisation of the Memorandum

The remainder of this Memorandum is organised into four parts:

<u>Part 1</u> gives general advice on when and where to make a video recording for criminal proceedings and sets out the legal conditions which must be satisfied before a criminal court can accept a video recording of an interview with a child witness. Part 1 also sets out some general considerations about suitable equipment. *The advice in Part 1 is of general validity and should be considered carefully by all those making video recorded interviews for criminal proceedings.*

<u>Part 2</u> gives advice about what should be done before the interview and sets out basic questions which should be addressed by those in the planning team. *Much of the advice in Part 2 relates to the specific circumstances of the interview, the child, and the human resources available for planning and conducting the interview. The advice in this Part will therefore need to be applied in the light of those circumstances.*

<u>Part 3</u>, on conduct of the interview, is divided into two chapters. The first sets out a protocol for interviewing children. The second chapter outlines the legal rules which should, so far as is possible, be observed in order to produce an evidentially acceptable video recording. *The principles underpinning both chapters are very important and all those planning and conducting interviews will need to have a sound grasp of them. However, their precise application will depend on individual circumstances. The methods in Part 3A are not recommended as the only, or necessarily the best, for all cases.*

The final part of the Memorandum, <u>Part 4</u>, gives guidance about matters which need to be dealt with once the video recording has been made, including arrangements for the proper storage, custody and disposal of tapes. *The guidance in Part 4 should be strictly adhered to in all cases.*

---

[5]Information about interviewing children for civil proceedings may be found in "Working Together" (see footnote 3 above) and, in respect of sexual abuse, "Interviewing Children Suspected of Being Sexually Abused. A Review of Theory and Practice" Vizard, E. (1991) in Clinical Approaches to Sex Offenders and their Victims, edited by Hollin, C.R. and Howell, K, John Wiley & Son Ltd., pp 17 – 148.

PART 1

GENERAL REQUIREMENTS

1.1   This part of the Memorandum first sets out legal conditions which must be satisfied before a criminal court can accept a video recording of an interview with a child witness. It then gives general guidance about when video recordings should be made in relation to a reported offence, appropriate locations, and the kind of equipment which is likely to produce video recordings acceptable to the court.

Requirements of the Criminal Justice Act 1988

1.2   Video recorded interviews with children may be admitted in a criminal trial under section 32A of the Criminal Justice Act 1988, (as added by the Criminal Justice Act 1991). A copy of section 32A is at annex B.

The new law is applicable if the child is not the accused...

1.3   Section 32A allows a video recording of an interview with a child witness of certain sexual or violent offences to be used, where it relates to any matter in issue in the proceedings, in trials at the *Crown Court*[1] or a *youth court*[1] Under section 32A a video recording is admissible only where:

(a)   the child is not the accused;

..and is available for cross-examination

(b)   the child is available for cross-examination (assuming the proceedings get that far); and

..and if the court has enough information about how the video was made

(c)   rules of court requiring disclosure of the circumstances in which the recording was made have been properly complied with.

1.4   The offences to which section 32 applies are:

(a)   any offence which involves assault on, or injury or a threat of injury to, a person;

(b)   an offence under section 1 of the Children and Young Persons Act 1933 (cruelty to persons under 16);

The Act covers violent and sexual offences

(c)   [2] any offence under the Sexual Offences Act 1956, the Indecency with Children Act 1960, the Sexual Offences Act 1967, section 54 of the Criminal Law Act 1977 or the Protection of Children Act 1978; and

(d)   any offence which consists of attempting or conspiring to commit, or of aiding, abetting, counselling, procuring or inciting the commission of, an offence falling within (a), (b) or (c) above.

1.5   *Examples of the information likely to be needed by the court to establish that such an offence was committed is set out in annex D.*

1.6   The upper[3] age limits of the child witnesses to whom section 32A applies are:

---

[1]See annexes A and B and Part 2 paragraph 2.16.
[2]A full list of these sexual offences is at annex C.
[3]There is no lower age limit.

(i)   in the case of any of the offences of violence or cruelty listed at (a) or (b) in paragraph 1.4, a person who is under fourteen years of age when the video recording was made, and is under fifteen years of age at the time of the trial; and

(ii) in the case of one of the sexual offences listed at (c) in paragraph 1.4, a person who is under seventeen years of age when the video recording was made, and is under eighteen years of age at the time of the trial.

When to make a video recording for criminal proceedings

1.7   The video recorded interview which is to be admissible in court should broadly equate with a witness statement of the first detailed account given to the police and should be conducted as soon as is practicable. Sufficient time must, however, be allowed for proper inter-agency consultation and planning (see Part 2 of this Code) as well as for any medical examination where that is appropriate. It is very important that the agencies involved have an opportunity to consider the child's needs, the legal context, possible civil proceedings, and the various implications of the interview before it takes place so that clear objectives for the interview can be agreed upon. *Video recorded interviews conducted in advance of this process are likely to be of very limited value, and may well compromise the usefulness of any later interviews.*

1.8   The need to consider a criminal investigation in a child care case may not immediately be apparent and it is possible that some initial questioning may have taken place before the police are involved. Any early discussions with the child should, so far as possible, adhere to the following basic principles:

A   *Listen to the child, rather than directly question him or her*

B   *Never stop a child who is freely recalling significant events*

C   *Make a note of the discussion, taking care to record the timing, setting and personnel present as well as what was said*

D   *Record all subsequent events up to the time of the substantive interview*

The child can be informed about the substantive interview as soon as it is planned. It will be important to avoid any coaching of the child for the interview, but answering his or her questions about the reasons for the interview would be helpful and would provide an opportunity to assess the child's willingness to be video recorded (see Part 2 paragraph 2.29).

1.9   Once it becomes clear that a criminal offence may have been committed an interview should be arranged, as soon as is practicable and consistent with adequate consultation and planning. Once a plan of action has been agreed upon it is vital to proceed quickly. This will minimise the stress experienced by the child and reduce the risk of him or her forgetting important details, or being influenced by others. It will also enable the accused person to be acquainted with the allegations made against him or her at an early stage.

1.10   In exceptional cases, for example where any deferment will occasion serious risk to the child, or when the alleged abuser has already been detained by the police, it might be necessary for an interview to be conducted immediately. In such cases there should be a clear record of the justification for proceeding in that way, since this information may be required by the court. *In the event of criminal proceedings, notes relating to the preparation and conduct of the video recorded interview will need to be disclosed to the Crown Prosecution Service together with the records of any other, perhaps informal, interviews with the child.*

Don't conduct further interviews unless you really have to

1.11 Once the video recorded interview has been completed no further questioning should take place unless the joint investigating team is fully satisfied, in consultation as necessary with the Crown Prosecution Service, that it is essential to elicit further information (see also Part 3A, paragraphs 3.41 to 3.44). Supplementary interviews should normally also be video recorded.

Where to make a video recording

Look for privacy, comfort and quiet

1.12 Careful consideration should be given to the selection of a suitable and sympathetic setting for the interview. The location should be private, quiet, reasonably comfortable and adequately equipped (but not over-equipped) for the interview. A private residence should not necessarily be ruled out (although the possible inhibiting effect of a home environment will need to be taken into account).

Choose a purpose-built facility if one is convenient

1.13 Video recorded interviews made at a facility designed for the purpose are likely to achieve the best quality results. In some areas, purpose-built interview suites are available at hospitals, family centres and similar places where children and other vulnerable witnesses such as rape victims may be interviewed. Such facilities will not always be readily accessible, especially from remote or rural areas, and the adverse effect and inconvenience to the child of a lengthy journey should be carefully considered against the possible lower quality of more readily available facilities.

Consider providing refreshment, lavatory, toys and games, and facilities for those with disabilities

1.14 The interview location should provide convenient and comfortable waiting areas and refreshment and lavatory facilities for the child and any accompanying adult. Some children will require wheelchair access to the interview room and other facilities, and those with a hearing disability may require an induction loop. (The needs of the disabled should be taken into account when setting up any new facilities). If appropriate, toys and games of a neutral kind (genitalled dolls are unsuitable) should be made available in the waiting area.

1.15 Where alternative locations exist, a final decision on where to hold the interview might need to be deferred until the needs of the particular child have been considered by the joint investigating team in the context of the detailed planning for the interview (see Part 2).

Do not use suspect interview rooms

1.16 Although police stations may have facilities for video recording interviews, they are not desirable locations for interviewing child victims or witnesses of sexual or other abuse. Such interviews should certainly never be held in interview rooms normally used for suspects.

What equipment to use

In principle you can use any equipment...

1.17 The relevant legislation[4] does not prescribe any particular equipment for use in video recorded interviews. In principle, a video recording of a child witness's testimony is admissible in court whatever equipment was used to make it. However, as explained in the Introduction, the court has power to reject all or part of the recording if it considers that it would not be in the interests of justice, or if it is not satisfied that it has the information specified in the relevant rules of court about the circumstances in which the recording was made.

...but it may be harder to get the video accepted in court with some equipment

1.18 The relevant Crown Court rules and the rules in respect of youth courts indicate that the court will require a good deal of information about the circumstances in which the interview took place. The use of equipment with certain technical features could make it easier to provide that information.

---

[4]See annexes B and E.

Aim for the standard which closed circuit TV gives in the court room

1.19   It should also be borne in mind that the video recording is intended to take the place of the giving in open court of certain oral testimony. In deciding whether the interests of justice would be served by admitting the video recording the court may consider the faithfulness to life of the record it provides. Admissibility could be jeopardised by the use of inadequate equipment.

1.20   The general rule which should guide choices about equipment is that it should be capable of reproducing, so far as is practicable and allowing for inherent differences between the quality of relayed and recorded images, what the court would see and hear if the child were giving his or her evidence via a live television link in a typical court room.[5]

1.21   The equipment will therefore need to be of good quality. It must be capable of capturing all the words and most, if not all, of the gestures or facial expressions of the witness and, ideally, should provide a view of the room and those in it. Guidance on suitable equipment and on the dimensions and furnishings of rooms suitable for these purposes is contained in annex F.

---

[5]When live television links are used in Crown Court trials, the judge sees on his monitor not only the child but also, from a second camera, the room from which the child is giving testimony and thus any accompanying person (see annex A for an explanation of live television links).

PART 2

BEFORE THE INTERVIEW

Planning is essential

2.1   No interview should be conducted without adequate planning. Even on the rare occasions when an interview must be conducted within hours, a plan including clearly defined objectives should still be prepared which draws on all the skills and experience of the disciplines represented on the joint investigating team. Failure to do so is likely to lead to an unsuccessful interview and consequent disservice to the interests of both the child and justice. Paragraphs 2.3 to 2.31 suggest several key areas which should be addressed during preparation of the plan. This is not a comprehensive check-list and each team should develop its own agenda in the light of its experience or knowledge of the individual child and all other relevant circumstances.

Look at the needs of the child and at certain legal points

2.2   This part of the Memorandum assumes that the child and the alleged offence will satisfy the basic legal conditions set out in Part 1, paragraphs 1.2 to 1.6. It also assumes that the team understands what information is needed in criminal proceedings to establish that a particular offence occurred (see annex D). It may be useful to have in mind a check-list of questions appropriate to the particular case. This check-list should be formulated during the preparation stage, drawing on the information available to the joint investigating team about the alleged offence(s) and the child's circumstances. If a full account of the nature of the offence(s) can be obtained it may save the child from having to undergo a supplementary interview (see Part 1, paragraph 1.11). The other legal matters which can best be addressed in the context of detailed consideration of the child's development and needs are *competence*[1], *compellability*[1] and the *likely availability of the child for cross-examination*[1]. These issues are addressed in paragraphs 2.11 to 2.16.

What developmental factors should the interviewing team consider?

Assess the child's development,...

2.3   The joint investigating team should note the child's chronological age and then assess the apparent developmental stage the child has reached, taking an overview of cognitive, linguistic, emotional, social, sexual, physical and other development, and the child's attention span. Professional help, for example from an educational psychologist or a teacher, may be valuable to the team. However, the potential benefits and the implications for delay of consulting other experts should be carefully weighed. Children of the same age can differ widely in their development, particularly if they have been abused or neglected. Information on these issues may have an important bearing on necessary preliminary decisions about the structure, style, duration and pace which are appropriate for the interview (See Part 1, paragraph 1.8, however, on the importance of avoiding any coaching of the child).

..use of language,...

2.4   Knowledge of the child's linguistic development is particularly important to enable the joint investigating team to plan how best to communicate with the child. Younger children are likely to have a limited vocabulary and language style and may use words and phrases

---

[1]See annex A

not in common parlance, particularly in relation to sexual activity and genitals. The interviewer will need to listen to the child and to adjust his or her language accordingly. It will help him or her to interview effectively if some informed consideration has been given to this aspect in advance of the interview.

...social and sexual understanding,...

2.5   Information about natural stages of developments[2] such as self-exploratory play and symbolic games may help the interviewer to determine when a child is behaving oddly. With older children, falsely adult behaviour is often one of the side effects of the experience of sexual abuse. Similarly, information about the child's knowledge of loving relationships and sexuality and what are and are not acceptable ways of expressing these may be available and relevant to the interview.

...concept of time...

2.6   The joint investigating team should take careful note of any available information about the child's understanding of the concept of time. Children, like adults, will usually find it easier to relate events to specific anniversaries and occasions than to refer to dates (see also Part 3A, paragraph 3.27).

...and ideas about trust

2.7   It will be useful to know in advance about the child's stage of development with regard to trust and the sharing of information. In the pre-school and early school years, great emphasis is placed on trusting adults to meet the child's needs. This goes with the concept of keeping one's word, not letting other people down and telling the truth. Keeping information to oneself is often linked with positive events in a child's life such as not telling someone what you are going to give them for their birthday. The interviewer must be aware of the possible pressure on a child who has promised to keep a secret.

Consider also the child's present state of mind,...

2.8   An appreciation of the likely state of the child's mind at the time of the interview will also help the joint investigating team to help the interviewer. Recalling certain events may cause a sudden change in behaviour or emotional state in the child. Guilt feelings may be present if the child feels he or she should have 'told' before, or feels that he or she is responsible for breaking up the family. Repeated child abuse can result in severe emotional and behavioural disturbance. Children may also react to the investigative process itself because it is unfamiliar, and aspects such as a medical examination or personal questions may be particularly upsetting for the child.

...cultural background...

2.9   The joint investigating team should also consider whether there are any special factors arising from the child's cultural or religious background which are relevant to planning an effective interview. In some cases it will be necessary for the team to seek advice in advance about particular ethnic customs and beliefs. Consideration of race, language, and also gender may influence the choice of interviewer. *A child should be interviewed in his or her first language except in the most exceptional circumstances.*

...and any disabilities

2.10   If the child has any disabilities, for example a speech or hearing impediment, or learning difficulties, particular care should be taken to develop effective strategies for the interview to minimise the effect of such disabilities. The use of dolls and other 'props' as communication aids should be considered (see Appendix I). In some cases it may be necessary for communication to pass through an appropriately skilled third party, for example a person who can use sign language. In others it might be necessary to consider asking such people to conduct the interview (see paragraph 2.24). As when any other language is used, a translation will need to be made available to the court.

---

[2]See, for example, "Protecting Children – A Guide for Social Workers Undertaking a Comprehensive Assessment", HMSO 1988.

Competence, compellability and availability for cross-examination

Will the court be able to make sense of what the child says?

2.11   The joint investigating team should consider, in the light of discussion of the child's development and needs whether, in principle, the child is likely to be able to give a coherent account of the events under investigation.

2.12   A video which is shown as evidence in a criminal trial will be able to speak to the court of any fact related by the child of which the child could have given evidence in person. The issue of the competence of a child may therefore arise in relation to a video recording.

Young children in general are no longer presumed incompetent withnesses; but at the trial an individual child might still not be competent to give evidence

2.13   Under the law as it existed before the 1991 Act, young children were assumed to be incompetent witnesses unless the contrary was proved. Before declaring a child to be competent, a court would require to be satisfied that the child was of sufficient intelligence to understand the difference between truth and lies, and the particular importance of telling the truth when giving evidence. Under the 1991 Act this restriction disappears: a child is no longer assumed to be incompetent and there is no duty on the court to examine the child as to competency before the trial. But it may still be the case, as it is with some adult witnesses, that a particular child proves to be unable to give an understandable account of the event under investigation. If this happens, that child's evidence will not be allowed to form part of the case for either the prosecution or the defence.

If the team can understand the child, assume the court will be able to also

2.14   It is not possible to predict precisely how the courts will treat the question of competence, if it is raised, in cases involving child witnesses following the 1991 Act. For the present, and in view of Parliament's clear intentions in reforming the law, it is suggested that *joint investigating teams should assume that the courts will be willing to listen to the evidence of any child who is able to communicate about the alleged offence in a way the team as a whole can understand.*

2.15   It should be noted that any child who is assumed to be *competent* under the 1991 Act will also be *compellable*. But this means only that a child who is wanted as a witness in court could be ordered to attend. It does *not* mean that, where the child is a witness for the prosecution, the Crown Prosecution Service will insist on including the evidence of a child in every case in which it is known that a child has provided some information to the police. In deciding whether to include a child's evidence, and whether it is in the public interest that a case should be brought to trial at all, the Crown Prosecution Service will take into account the interests and wishes of the child. Reports to the Crown Prosecution Service should always include clear information about the wishes of the child, and his or her parents or carers, about going to court. The Crown Prosecution Service may in any event need to seek further information from the joint investigating team.

The child must be available for cross-examination

2.16   As explained in Part 1, paragraph 1.3, section 32A of the Criminal Justice Act 1988 (as added by the 1991 Act) states that a video recording is not admissible unless the child is available for cross-examination. What that means is that, if the accused person pleads not guilty, he or she must have the opportunity to have the evidence against him or her tested in court. Under the 1991 Act the accused will *not* be allowed to question the child in person[3]; and the child will be eligible to apply to give evidence from outside the courtroom via a live

---

[3]See section 34A of the Criminal Justice Act 1988 (as added by the Criminal Justice Act 1991)

television link[4]. However, the child must be available to be questioned by the judge and by the legal representatives of the parties. If the joint investigating team concludes that there is no reasonable expectation whatever that the particular child can be made available for those purposes then they should consider, in consultation with the Crown Prosecution Service, whether it may still be possible to use a video recording in evidence under other provisions in the Criminal Justice Act 1988. A brief description of the alternative provisions is given at annex G.

But even if the child cannot be cross-examined, the video recording might still be used

What should be the duration of the interview and its pace?

Plan the length of the interview

2.17   It is important that the team should plan in advance the expected duration of the interview. It will help both the interviewer and the child to have a clear idea of how long the interview is likely to last. It is not possible to say how long an average interview will take. This will depend on the age of the child, his or her attention span and any other particular intellectual or physical limitations. As a rule of thumb, the team should plan the interview to last for less than an hour (excluding breaks – see paragraph 2.19) unless they have good reason to believe that the child is mature and strong enough to cope with longer. It is recognised that there will, of course, be cases where the child has experienced abuse over long periods and that such accounts may take a considerable time to narrate. In addition, the child's actual state and needs during the course of the interview may suggest that the original planned duration needs to be revised. Nothing in the foregoing is intended to preclude a child from giving a lengthy account of relevant details but interviewers should always be mindful of the needs of the child and earlier considerations should not lightly be set aside, particularly if the inclination is to extend the interview.

The child should dictate the pace of the interview, not the interviewer

2.18   The basic rule is that the interview should go at the pace of the child and not of the adult. *Those more used to interviewing adults will need to be especially careful not to go too fast for the child or to seem impatient.* On the other hand, *those with experience mainly in child care might go too slowly and, for example, tend to dwell in the "rapport" phase* (see Part 3A, paragraphs 3.4 to 3.11) when the child is ready to proceed to the next phase of the interview. An accompanying person (see paragraph 2.26) can usefully observe the effect of the interview on the child. He or she can discreetly guide the interviewer by use of a pre-arranged signal if it appears that the child is finding the experience oppressive or appears to be acceding to what he or she perceives to be the demands of the situation in order to bring it to an end.

Breaks may be necessary

2.19   At appropriate intervals during the interview the child may need to be offered a break to go to the lavatory (particularly as anxiety can increase the need to relieve oneself) or for refreshment, but the latter should not appear to be offered as a reward for co-operation.

2.20   If the interview is not continuous, the reasons for any interruption should be carefully noted, together with a record of what occurred during any interval(s), including all periods away from the interviewing facility. It may be important to be able to demonstrate that the child was not prompted or coached between interviews. It will be difficult to keep a proper record if the interview is spread over more than one day, and it is therefore strongly recommended that interviews are conducted on one day if at all possible.

Take account of the child's normal routine

2.21   In considering the timing of the interview the joint investigating team should take into account such factors as the child's normal bed-

---

[4]By virtue of section 32(1)(b) of the 1988 Act (as amended), where a video recording is to be played in place of the child's evidence in chief, that child will also be eligible to give evidence via a live television link from outside the courtroom. This facility is granted at the judge's discretion, which is exercised positively in nearly all cases.

time and the general needs of the child and those who care for him or her.

Who should be the interviewer?

2.22   The investigating team should consider, in the light of the issues outlined in the preceding sections, who appears best qualified to conduct the interview and who, if anyone, should accompany that person. A special blend of skills is required to interview children effectively for evidential purposes.

The interviewer should be adept in dealing with the child *and* understand the legal constraints

2.23   The interviewer should be a person who has, or is likely to be able to establish, rapport with the child, who understands how to communicate effectively with him or her, including in sometimes disturbed periods, and who also has a proper grasp both of the basic rules of evidence and the elements of criminal offences. This is a formidable job specification and some compromise will probably be necessary. A rigid definition of the roles of police and social service professionals is not likely to be possible or desirable and a high degree of flexibility and responsiveness within the joint investigating team is required in the interests of an effective interview.

2.24   Exceptionally, it may be in the interests of the child to be interviewed by an adult in whom he or she has already put confidence but who is not a member of the investigating team. Provided that such a person is not a party to the proceedings, is prepared to co-operate with appropriately trained interviewers and can accept adequate briefing this possibility should not be precluded.

The interviewer may well be required to give evidence in court

2.25   The interviewer should also be prepared to testify about the interview in court if called upon to do so. He or she, or any person connected with the interview, may be questioned about the conduct of the interview and events surrounding it. *Careful notes should therefore be kept.* A statement dealing with the preparation and conduct of the interview should be made whilst the events are still fresh in the interviewer's mind.

The interviewer may need some help

2.26   It will be helpful if a second member of the investigating team is available to accompany the interviewer. He or she can help to ensure that the interview will be conducted in a professional manner, by discreetly suggesting supplementary questions at appropriate times, and by taking notes which can be useful within the interview (see Part 3A, paragraph 3.2). The initial nomination about who should take the lead can be reconsidered during the interview (see Part 3A, paragraph 3.4). It is desirable that the child should be questioned by only one person during any phase of the interview.

Who else should be present during the interview?

Normally, no-one else should be in the room

2.27   Limiting the number of people present at the interview should lessen the possibility of the child feeling overwhelmed by the situation and uncomfortable about revealing information. *A suspected offender should never be present.* The presence of other people may also distract or put pressure upon the child. The court, in considering whether to admit the recording, may wish to be assured that the witness was not prompted or discouraged during the interview, and to provide a comprehensive record of the words and gestures of more than two persons can be technically demanding (see annex F). However, such considerations may be outweighed by the benefit of having a supportive accompanying adult available to comfort and reassure a very young or distressed child, particularly if the child requests it. In such cases the accompanying adult will need to be clear that he or she must take no part in the interview.

2.28   Where a person accompanying the child (for example an "appropriate adult" as mentioned in the Codes of Practice accompanying the Police and Criminal Evidence Act 1984) is to monitor the interview, this could be achieved from the equipment control room if there is one.

Does the child need to agree to be video recorded?

Seek the child's agreement to video recording

2.29   Where a child is mature enough to understand the concept, he or she should be given an explanation of the purpose of the video recording so that the child is fully informed to a level appropriate to his or her age and understanding and freely consents to the interview session and the video recording. It should be explained that the video recording may be shown to the court instead of the child giving his or her account directly. The child should be advised that, whether a video recording is made or not, he or she may be required to attend court to answer questions directly. *Written consent to be video recorded is not necessary*[5] but it is unlikely to be practicable or desirable to video record an interview with a reluctant or distressed child.

2.30   When the child is too young to understand fully, the team should listen to the views of the parent or carers. However they should guard against the possibility of anyone who may be implicated in abuse of the child exerting any pressure on the child not to give his or her account.

2.31   A specimen information sheet to be handed to the child's parent or carer, is at annex H. An information pack for child witnesses and their parents/carers is being developed by Government departments in conjunction with the voluntary sector and will be made available during 1992.

---

[5]Existing Home Office guidelines to the police on the investigation of sexual offences against children contain a specimen consent form for parents to complete where it is proposed to video record an interview with a child. The use of this form is no longer recommended except where consent would be necessary if the interview were not recorded.

CONDUCTING THE INTERVIEW – THE BASIC APPROACH

The purpose of the interview is to discover what, if anything, happened

3.1   The basic aim of the interview is to obtain a truthful account from the child, in a way which is fair and in the child's interests and acceptable to the courts. What follows is a recommended protocol for interviewing based on a phased approach. This treats the interview as a process in which a variety of interviewing techniques are deployed in relatively discrete phases, proceeding from general and open to specific and closed forms of question. It is suggested that this approach is likely to achieve the basic aim of listening to what the child has to say, if anything, about the alleged offence. However, inclusion of a phased approach in this Memorandum should not be taken to imply that all other techniques are necessarily unacceptable or to preclude their development. Neither should what follows be regarded as a check-list to be rigidly worked through. Nevertheless, the sound legal framework it provides should not be departed from by members of joint investigating teams unless they have fully discussed and agreed the reasons for doing so and have consulted their senior managers.

Only one person should speak to the child

3.2   *Normally*, only the interviewer should speak to the child throughout the interview. The accompanying person, if there is one, may helpfully indicate supplementary or follow-up approaches using an unobtrusive pre-arranged procedure. Use of a radio controlled earpiece may be helpful. (See also Part 2, paragraphs 2.18 and 2.26).

Preliminaries

Check the equipment

Introduce everyone to the child

State date and time

3.3   The interviewer should be satisfied that the equipment is working properly and that lighting and audio facilities are appropriate. This should be done before the child is brought into the room. For the benefit of the court[1] and the child, at the the start of the recording the interviewer should introduce all those present to the child, using the name the child prefers to be known by. He or she should state the date and time at the beginning and end of each session. If only one camera is used, the location and what is going on in the room will also need to be described. The child should be encouraged to sit or, if the circumstances demand it, play in the area covered by the video camera.

Phase One – Rapport

The rapport phase helps the child to relax and the interviewer to make further decisions about the interview

3.4   The main aim of the first phase of the interview is to build up a rapport between the interviewer and the child in which the child is helped to relax and feel as comfortable as possible in the interview situation. However, this phase serves a number of important additional functions. If used correctly, it should supplement the interviewer's knowledge about the child's social, emotional and cognitive

---

[1]See Part 1 paragraph 1.17 and annex E.

development, and particularly about his or her communication skills and degree of understanding (for example, the number of words used by the child in sentences might cause the interviewer to revise an earlier judgement about the most suitable length of questions). The rapport phase can also indicate a need to review an initial decision about which of two possible interviewers should take the lead. *A rapport phase, however brief, should not be omitted even if the child has had significant previous contact with the interviewer.*

Don't refer to the alleged offence

3.5 The alleged offence and related topics should *not* be referred to during the rapport phase. Typically, the child is led into free discussion of non-related events in his or her life, such as school, play group, the journey[2] to the interview, or favourite television programmes. The rapport phase should be tailored to the needs and circumstances of the individual child. With younger children a rapport phase may involve some play with toys, drawing or colouring to help the child relax and or to interact with the interviewer. (Such play should *not* be used during this phase to gather information relevant to the alleged offence).

Play is acceptable

Don't stare or touch the child

3.6 Whatever technique is used, the interviewer should be careful here and throughout the interview not to overemphasise his or her authority in relation to the child. The interviewer should also avoid staring continuously at the child, or touching the child in any way which might recall abuse.

Explain the reason for the interview

3.7 At some early point during the rapport phase the reason for the interview should be briefly explained in a way that takes account of the child's needs, and which does not refer to the alleged offence. The approach to this will depend not only on the child's level of understanding but also on whether, prior to the interview, the child has given any direct intimation of abuse having taken place. It will be permissible for the interviewer to say that he or she wants to talk about something the child has told someone else but the interviewer should not mention the substance of the previous disclosure. If no such disclosure has been made the interviewer might say that he or she wished to talk to the child because something seemed to be making the child unhappy. (Once the reason for the interview has been explained some children will follow on naturally to a free narrative account (Phase Two) at this point.)

Be reassuring

3.8 The interviewer should bear in mind that some children will assume that because they are being interviewed, they must have done something wrong. The interviewer might need to reassure the child on this point but promises or predictions should not be made about the likely outcome of the interview. So far as possible, the interview should be conducted in a "neutral" atmosphere, with the interviewer taking care not to assume, or appear to assume, the guilt of an individual whose alleged conduct may be the subject of the interview.

Show the child the camera

3.9 The existence of the video camera should also be drawn to the attention of the child. A younger child may be reassured by the explanation that what he or she says may need to be heard by other adults in order that they can help the interviewer to decide how best to help the child. An older child may be relieved by the more direct explanation that the interview is being recorded so he or she will not need to keep repeating his or her account.

Explain the ground rules for discussion

3.10 Before the child is invited to volunteer information about the alleged offences, the interviewer should consider initiating a short discussion in which he or she can *convey to the child the need to speak the truth and the acceptability of saying 'I don't know' or 'I don't understand'.* There is no legal requirement to administer the oath or admonish the child but since the video recording may be used in court as the child's

---

[2]Mention of the child's home address should be avoided if possible as such information might need to be edited out for court proceedings.

16

evidence, it will be helpful for the court to know that the child was made aware of the need to tell the truth. The interviewer should use terms suitable to the child's age, understanding and emotional condition. Some child witnesses may fear that their truthful accounts will not be believed. An insensitive approach could confirm that fear. Explaining to the child the need to tell the truth later in the interview is not recommended because it might risk the child concluding that the interviewer has not believed what he or she has said so far about the event.

3.11   One form of words would be *"Please tell [us] all you can remember. Don't make anything up or leave anything out. This is very important"*. Or the interviewer could complete an age-appropriate discussion with the child of what is true and false by saying something like: *"You can tell me anything you want. I don't want you to feel you need hold anything back. All that matters is that you don't make anything up or leave anything out."*

Phase Two – Free Narrative Account

Encourage the child to speak freely and spontaneously

3.12   Having asked the child to speak truthfully and re-established rapport, if necessary, the child should then be encouraged to provide *in his or her own words* and at his or her own pace an account of the relevant event(s). This is the heart of the interview and the interviewer's role is to act as a facilitator, not an interrogator. Only the most general, open-ended questions should be asked in this phase, for example: *"Why do you think we are here today?"; "Is there anything that you would like to tell me?"* If the child responds in a positive way to such questions then the interviewer can encourage the child to give a free narrative account of events. Every effort must be made to obtain information from the child which is spontaneous and free from the interviewer's influence.

Only ask about information mentioned by the child

3.13   In this free narrative phase the interviewer should encourage the child to provide an account in his or her own words by the use of appropriate open-ended prompts such as "Did anything else happen?". Verbs like "tell" and "explain" are likely to be useful. The prompts used at this stage should *not* include information known to the interviewer concerning relevant events which have not yet been mentioned by the child. Prompts should not be over-used.

3.14   The interviewer should keep in mind that many children will feel uncomfortable about recalling some events and will move slowly from peripheral matters. They may need reassurance, for example "I can see you are finding this difficult, but you are being very brave. Just keep telling us about it and we will listen." Research has also confirmed that younger children are usually able to provide less information in their narrative accounts than do older children and adults. Nevertheless, such information is considered to be typically no less accurate. Moreover, it is younger children whose accounts are probably most tainted by inappropriate questioning.

Be patient with the child

3.15   In all cases, the interviewer should resist the temptation to speak as soon as the child appears to stop doing so. The interviewer should be tolerant of pauses, including long ones, and silences. The interviewer should also be tolerant of what may appear to be irrelevant or repetitious information from the child. Above all, the interviewer must try to curb any eagerness to determine whether the child witnessed the alleged offence. A form of 'active listening' is needed, letting the child know that what he or she has said has been heard by the interviewer and reflecting this back in the child's own words, for example: "I didn't like it when he did that." (child) "You didn't like it?" (adult). The interviewer should be aware of the danger of consciously or subconsciously indicating by inflexion of the voice, approval or disapproval of the answer just given.

If nothing of relevance emerges during this phase, consider closing the interview

3.16   If the child has said nothing at all relevant to the alleged offence(s) the interviewer should consider, in the light of the plans made for the interview and in consultation as necessary with the accompanying person, whether to proceed to the next phase of the interview. The needs of the child and those of justice must both be considered. Exceptionally, consideration may be given to concluding the interview, moving directly to Phase Four (see paragraphs 3.36 to 3.39).

Phase Three – Questioning

(A)   Open-ended questions

Begin the questioning with open-ended questions

3.17   The first stage of Phase Three involves open-ended questions which ask the child to provide more information but in a way that does not lead the child or put him or her under pressure. However, as with all questions used in the interview, *it should always be clear to the child that to reply "I can't remember" or "I don't know" is perfectly acceptable.* The child should also be encouraged to say if he or she does not understand a question.

3.18   With younger children the interviewer may need to say, in simple terms, that he or she has no idea what has happened to them. Very young children often assume that because one adult knows what has happened to them, other adults are somehow privy to this knowledge.

Ask only one question at a time and don't use confusing grammar

3.19   For a child who has provided very little relevant information in the free narrative phase a focused yet open-ended question could be of the form "Are there some things you are not very happy about?" Only one question should be asked at a time. Simple sentence construction should be used, avoiding double negatives and other potentially confusing forms of language. *It is particularly important in such cases to proceed through this phase step by step and not be tempted to get to what he or she may consider to be the heart of the matter by asking what a court may later consider to be prejudicial leading questions.*

3.20   For a child whose free narrative account provided somewhat more relevant information, the questions could be more focused but should still be open-ended, for example "Could you please tell me more about the man in the park who frightened you?" (assuming that *the child* has mentioned a frightening man in the park). If the child becomes distressed when questioned even in this non-leading way, the interviewer should move away from the subject and consider reverting to an earlier phase of the interview (for example, re-establish through rapport that the child is at ease). Such shifting away from and then back to a topic the child finds difficult may be required several times in an interview.

3.21   If the child has mentioned being the victim of or witnessing sexual or physical abuse during the free narrative account, it will be important to try to establish whether this was a single event or whether repeated abuse has occurred. This is necessary not only for evidential purposes, but also to guide any further questioning of the child. Younger children's free narrative accounts (or their earlier words on the relevant matter) may well be less specific than older children's. Moreover, if abuse occurred repeatedly some children may find it difficult to recall specific episodes before the general pattern has been described.

3.22   Some questions beginning with 'why' may be interpreted by children as attributing blame or guilt to them. Repeating a question soon after a child has answered should also be avoided since this may be interpreted by children as a criticism of their original response. Research shows that persistent repetition of a question may lead a child to give an answer he or she believes the interviewer wants to hear.

18

Don't interrupt the child, even if the language used is unclear

3.23 It is also important to avoid interrupting the child. If, for example, the child has used obscure words for parts of the body, or for any other object/event/person, this should not normally be followed up immediately by a direct question to clarify meaning. The interviewer should carefully note the point and seek a suitable opportunity for clarification later in the interview.

(B) Specific yet non-leading questions

Specific but non-leading questions allow the interviewer to clarify earlier information

3.24 Before moving on to the next stage the interviewer should again consider whether it is in the interests of the child to do so. This stage allows for extension and clarification of previously provided information both from the free narrative and subsequent phase. It also provides an opportunity for the child who has said very little in connection with the purpose of the interview to be reminded of the focus of the interview without the child being asked leading questions (see paragraphs 3.33 to 3.35 and Part 3B paragraphs 3.51 to 3.55).

Don't use closed or leading questions yet

3.25 Adults sometimes wrongly suppose that children, even young ones, must know what is relevant. Being helped to understand what is relevant helps a witness to focus his or her account and specific yet non-leading questions should allow the interviewer to guide the witness in an evidentially sound manner. During this stage questions should not be leading to the extent that the question implies the answer although in some cases it may be inevitable that questions will refer to disputed facts. *However, during this stage questions which require a 'yes' or 'no' answer, or ones which allow only one of two possible responses, should not be asked.*

3.26 For example, for a child who has already provided information that a man in the park frightened her and that he was wearing a scarf, a specific yet non-leading question could be "What colour was the man's scarf?" (If the child responds with a colour and the interviewer has some reason to doubt that the child understands what it means, the interviewer could note the point and later in the interview it could be established that the child does, indeed, know what the response, for example, "lilac", means.)

Try to use language appropriate to the particular child

3.27 If the child's account so far has mentioned repeated abuse, but has not described in any, or sufficient, detail separate incidents, this may now be the time to try to clarify the point. In considering how best to help the child be more specific the interviewer should bear in mind that young children find it more difficult to remember events if adult-appropriate language is used in the questioning. For example, calendar dates or days of the week may be inappropriate. It may be more productive to refer to life events meaningful to the child, such as before or after Christmas/birthday/holiday; schoolday or non-schoolday. For time of day, mentioning meal times, television programmes, bedtime and the like could be useful. Interviewers should try to pick up on the 'labels' the child uses for various incidents and use these in the questioning.

Probe gently factual and linguistic inconsistencies

3.28 If inconsistencies have occurred in the child's account, they can be gently probed during this stage of the questioning. (The child should not be told directly that he or she has been inconsistent.) Similarly, if the child has displayed knowledge or surprising language apparently beyond his or her years (for example "I'm a good cock-sucker") the source of this could be established. If the child has described acts of sexual or physical abuse the interviewer could ask tactfully if the child has seen explicit films, videos, magazines or books, and if so, seek to establish whether the child has merely described these.

Ask if the child has told anyone else

3.29   If a child has apparently given an account of abuse for the first time, it would be useful to ask if he or she had tried to tell anyone about it before. However the interviewer should take care to avoid inadvertently attributing any blame or guilt to a child who has never previously felt able to disclose the facts.

(C)   Closed questions

More specific answers may be obtained using closed questions

3.30   If specific but non-leading questions are unproductive, questions might be attempted that give the child a limited number of alternative responses. For example "Was the man's scarf you mentioned blue or yellow, or another colour, or can't you remember?".

3.31   If such a question permits only one of two responses then the response may not necessarily be a good indication of what is in the memory, especially if the child is unwilling to give a "don't know" response and/or the interviewer has not established that as an acceptable reply. Such a limited question might not fall foul of the rule about leading questions (see Part 3B paragraph 3.51) but on the other hand it might not elicit a truly informative reply. It should also be remembered that if the answer given to a limited response question concerns a fact to be disputed in court, the question may then be considered to be leading.

3.32   At the end of this stage the interviewer may conclude that further questioning is necessary and that leading questions might be appropriate. However, it must be understood that a leading style of questioning may produce replies which are excluded from criminal proceedings.

(D)   Leading questions

Avoid leading questions

3.33   Put simply, a leading question is one which implies the answer or assumes facts which are likely to be in dispute (see Part 3B, paragraphs 3.51 to 3.55 for a fuller explanation). Leading questions would not normally be allowed if the child were giving his or her evidence in chief live during criminal proceedings and it is to be expected that such questioning in a video recorded interview would be excluded by the court. The greatest care must therefore be taken when questioning the child about central matters which are likely to be disputed.

Avoid questions which invariably require the same answer

3.34   In addition to the legal objections, psychological research indicates strongly that interviewees' responses to leading questions tend to be determined by the manner of questioning rather than valid recall. It seems likely that young children in particular may be more willing to respond to 'yes/no' questions with a 'yes' response. If, therefore, questions permitting only a 'yes' or 'no' response are asked in this phase, these should be phrased so that those on the same issue sometimes seek a 'yes' response and sometimes a 'no' response.

Go back to an earlier phase if new information emerges

3.35   It cannot be over-emphasised that responses to leading questions referring to central facts of the case that have not already been described by the child in an earlier phase of the interview are likely to be of very limited evidential value in criminal proceedings. If such a question produces an evidentially relevant response, particularly one which contains relevant information not led by the question, the interviewer should take care not to follow this up with further questions which might have the effect of "leading" the child. Instead he or she should revert to the "neutral" mode of questioning described earlier.

Phase Four – Closing the Interview

A closing phase is essential

Make sure the child is not distressed

3.36 Every interview should have a closing phase conducted in the interests of the child. It has already been emphasised that it may be appropriate to terminate an interview before sufficient information has been obtained from the child for criminal proceedings. In such circumstances, the child should not be made to feel that he or she has failed, or disappointed the interviewer. The interviewer should be careful to ensure that all interviews end appropriately. Every effort should be made to ensure that the child is not distressed but is in a positive frame of mind.

Go over the important parts again using the child's language

3.37 During this phase the interviewer may need to check with the child that he or she (the interviewer) has correctly understood the important parts, if any, of the child's account. If this is considered necessary, care should be taken not to convey disbelief. Any recapping should use the child's own language, *not* a summary provided by the interviewer in adult language (which could contain errors but with which the child may nevertheless agree).

Return to the rapport phase, if necessary

Thank the child and allow him/her to ask questions

3.38 It may then be appropriate to revert to some of the "neutral" topics mentioned in the rapport phase (see paragraph 3.5). The child should be thanked for his or her time and effort and asked if there is anything more he or she wishes to say. An explanation should be given to the child of what may happen next, but, again, promises which cannot be kept should not be made. The child should always be asked if he or she has any questions and these answered as appropriately as possible.

Give the child (or accompanying adult) a contact name and number

3.39 It is good practice to give to the child (or, if more appropriate, the accompanying adult) a contact name and telephone number in case the child later decides that he or she wishes to discuss further matters with the interviewer.

3.40 The following table provides a summary of the phased approach:

	Purpose	Approach	To be avoided	Additional comments
Phase I Rapport	To settle the child and relieve anxiety. To supplement interviewer's knowledge of child. To explain reason for interview. To admonish child to speak the truth.	Any topic which relaxes the child. Play may be needed.	Any mention of the alleged offence. Staring at or touching child at any time.	This phase may need to be repeated at several points in the interview. *Never* start without it.
Phase II Free Narrative Account	To enable child to give an account in own words.	Provide opportunities to talk about alleged offence at child's pace. Use a form of "active listening".	Questions directed to events not mentioned by child. Speaking as soon as child appears to stop.	Be patient. If nothing related to alleged offence is mentioned, consider moving to Phase IV.
Phase III Questioning	To find out more about alleged offence.	Questions graduating from general to more specific.	Interrupting the child even to clarify language. Repeating a question too soon. Using difficult grammar/ sentence construction. Asking more than one question at a time.	Consider at each stage of questioning whether it is in interests of child and justice to proceed further.
Stage A Open-ended questions	Enable child to provide more information without pressure.	Use focused but non-leading questions.		
Stage B Specific yet non-leading questions	To extend and clarify information. To remind child of purpose of interview.	Use specific questions which may inevitably refer to disputed facts. Probe factual and linguistic inconsistencies gently.	Questions which require a "yes" or "no" answer or allow only one of a possible two responses.	
Stage C Closed questions	To encourage reticent child to speak.	Questions which allow a limited number of responses.		Consult with other interviewer before questioning further.
Stage D Leading questions	To encourage reticent child to speak.	Questions can be used which imply answer or assume disputed facts.	Questions which invariably require same answer.	Avoid all directly leading questions. Revert to "neutral" mode as soon as possible, and in all cases in which an answer seems evidentially relevant.

	Purpose	Approach	To be avoided	Additional comments
Phase IV Closing the interview	To ensure child has understood interview and is not distressed.	Go over relevant evidence in child's language. Revert to rapport topics. Thank child and allow child to ask questions.	Summarising in adult language.	Never stop without it.Give child or accompanying adult contact name and number.

Further interviews

A further interview may be held if it is strictly necessary

3.41 One of the key aims of video recording early investigative interviews is to reduce the number of times a child is asked to tell his or her account. However, it may be the case that even with an experienced and skilful interviewer, the child may provide less information than he or she is capable of divulging. A supplementary interview may therefore be necessary (see Part 1, paragraph 1.11) and this, too, should be video recorded. Consideration should always be given to whether holding such an interview would be in the child's interest. In no circumstances should a supplementary interview for evidential purposes be conducted by members of joint investigation teams unless they are fully satisfied, in consultation as necessary with the Crown Prosecution Service, that a supplementary interview is needed.

Taking further evidence in writing is possible but not recommended

3.42 Taking further evidence in writing is not recommended. Any such written statement will not be automatically admitted in evidence and the child witness is likely to be required to repeat it at the trial.

3.43 The reasons for conducting a supplementary interview should be clearly articulated and recorded in writing. More than one supplementary interview is unlikely to be appropriate unless the joint investigating team makes the decision at the planning stage (see Part 2, paragraph 2.20) to divide the phases of an interview with a very young or psychologically disturbed child into a number of sections to be conducted by the same interviewer on different days, with rapport and closure being achieved each time.

Counselling could now take place

3.44 Once the video recorded interview is complete, it should be possible for appropriate counselling and therapy to take place. It should become standard practice to inform the police and the Crown Prosecution Service about the nature of any such therapy in each case. The defence may justifiably wish to know about both the nature and content of the therapy that has taken place before the child gives evidence in cross-examination.

APPENDIX I   USE OF DOLLS AND OTHER 'PROPS'

'Props' include dolls, drawings, dolls' houses and small figures which can serve as potentially very useful communication aids in interviews carried out for the purposes of this Memorandum. Young children and those with communication difficulties, may be able to provide clearer accounts when such props are used, compared with purely verbal approaches. For example, drawing or dolls may allow a child to demonstrate body parts or an abusive incident, while a doll's house may help the child to describe the environment in which an incident took place. All props should be used with caution and without leading questions. The need for their use should be carefully considered before the interview.

Particular care is necessary when genitalled dolls are used, where it is important that the interviewer is skilled and trained in their use and misuse. A combination of leading questioning style and the use of genitalled dolls can be particularly error prone, and is unlikely to produce evidence which could be used in criminal proceedings. In the main, genitalled dolls should only be used as an adjunct to the interview to establish the meaning of terms used by the child *once the child has finished his or her free narrative account, and the general substance or his or her evidence is reasonably clear.*

APPENDIX II   OTHER QUESTIONING TECHNIQUES

There are other methods of encouraging a child to give his or her account and these may also be used in interviews carried out for the purposes of this Memorandum *provided that the evidential considerations are borne in mind.*

A facilitative style of questioning may be used with children who are particularly reticent. This can involve asking the child about nice/nasty things, good/bad people, what the child would like to change in his or her life, or similar techniques. For those children who have been put under pressure not to disclose certain matters an open-ended discussion of secrets may be introduced.

Such methods may be very successful for those trained in such particular styles of questioning. If the interviewer avoids any suggestive questioning and succeeds in encouraging the child to give a spontaneous account there should be no reason why evidence gained in this way should not be acceptable to the courts. *However, such techniques should not be used without prior discussion and agreement with senior managers (see Part 3A, paragraph 3.1).*

It may happen that a child who is being interviewed comes under suspicion of involvement in a criminal offence, perhaps by uttering a self-incriminating statement. Although this is not expected to be a frequent occurrence, interviewers should bear in mind that it is not unusual for victims to become abusers.

If it is concluded that the evidence of the *child as suspect* is paramount in a particular case, the interview should be terminated so that any further questioning can be carried out in accordance with the relevant provisions of the Code for the Detention, Treatment and Questioning of Persons by Police Officers (PACE Code C). That Code provides, amongst other things, for the cautioning of a suspect and for the presence of an appropriate adult during questioning.

A child who incriminates him or herself in a criminal offence may ask the interviewer for some guarantee of immunity. On no account should any such guarantee be given to a child over the age of criminal responsibility (10 years), however remote the prospect of criminal proceedings against the child might seem. If the child is to be interviewed in accordance with PACE, he or she will be cautioned and the purpose of the interview will be made clear.

Where the priority is to obtain evidence from the *child as a victim or a witness* the interview can proceed and should follow the guidance in this Memorandum but it should be borne in mind that a video recorded interview conducted in this way is unlikely to be admissible in criminal proceedings brought *against* the child.

CONDUCTING THE INTERVIEW – THE LEGAL CONSTRAINTS

The video is subject to the rules of evidence

3.46   As explained in the Introduction to this Memorandum, the video recorded interview is intended to take the place of the first stage of the child's evidence in court. The video recording will count as evidence of any fact stated by the child of which he or she could have given evidence in court. This means that, in principle, the rules which govern procedure in court may be applied to the video recorded interview.

3.47   There are rules which can render certain matters 'inadmissible' irrespective of their truth, so that they cannot form part of the case. A criminal court has no power to depart from such rules. However there are also conventions of the court which the court may relax where the need arises. The most obvious example of such a convention is the avoidance of leading questions.

3.48   The court will not expect video recorded interviews with children exactly to mimic examination of a witness by counsel in court. But rules of evidence have been created in order to ensure a fair trial for the accused, and they cannot be ignored. Early consultation with the Crown Prosecution Service should assist in identifying potential areas of difficulty.

The interviewer should abide by the basic rules of evidence

3.49   It is therefore good practice to conduct an interview as far as possible in accordance with the rules which would apply in court. *Interviewers who ignore these rules are likely to produce video recordings which are unacceptable to a criminal court.* They will thus fail to spare the child from having to give the first stage of his or her evidence in person.

3.50   This Part of the Memorandum explains the rationale behind those rules most likely to affect a video recorded interview - *leading questions, previous statements showing consistency or truth, statements about the bad character of the accused.* As with most rules there are circumstances in which they need not be applied. This is easier to determine when a child is being questioned in court and counsel can agree at the time with the judge what is acceptable. The interviewer has no such opportunity and should therefore err on the side of caution but, as this Part goes on to describe, there are circumstances when the rules can properly be disregarded.

Leading questions

Courts can be expected to disallow questions which suggest the answer or assume disputed facts

3.51   It is not generally permissible to put leading questions to a witness. A leading question is one which either suggests the required answer, or which is based on an assumption of facts which have yet to be proved. Thus 'Daddy hurt you, didn't he?' is an example of the first type of leading question, and 'When did you first tell anyone about what Daddy did?', put to a child who has not yet alleged that Daddy did anything, is an example of the second type.

3.52   Where a leading question is improperly put to a witness in court, the answer is not inadmissible but may be accorded little or no weight because of the manner in which it was obtained. When witnesses testify live in court a leading question can be objected to before a witness replies. The party not tendering the video evidence has no such opportunity and so may ask for a part of the video recording to be edited out.

There are exceptions to the leading questions rule

3.53   However there are circumstances where leading questions are permissible:

> (a) A witness is often led into his or her testimony by being asked to confirm his or her name and address, or some other introductory matter because these *matters are unlikely to be in dispute.* More central issues may also be the subject of leading questions if there is no dispute about them. For example, where it is common ground that a person, X, has been killed at a particular time, it is not 'leading' to ask a witness 'What were you doing when X was killed?' However, at the interview stage it may not be known what facts will be in dispute at the trial and so it will be safer to assume that most matters are still in dispute.

> (b) The courts also accept that in cases other than the above it is *impractical to ban leading questions.* This may be because the subject-matter of the question is such that it cannot be put to the witness without leading, as for example when the witness is to be asked to identify the person who hurt him or her. Or it may be because the witness does not understand what he or she is expected to tell the court without some prompting, as in the case of a young child or a child with a learning difficulty.

But interviewers should avoid any leading questions except when strictly necessary

3.54   An interviewer who follows the provisions of this Memorandum as to the conduct of an interview (see Part 3A) will avoid leading questions. As the courts become more aware of the difficulties of obtaining evidence from witnesses who are very young or who have a learning difficulty, and of counteracting the pressures on child witnesses to keep silent, a sympathetic attitude may be taken towards *necessary* leading questions. A leading question which succeeds in prompting a child into providing information spontaneously beyond that led by the question will normally be acceptable. However, *unless there is absolutely no alternative,* the interviewer should never be the first to suggest to the child that a particular offence was committed, or that a particular person was responsible. Once this step has been taken it will be extremely difficult to counter the argument that the interviewer put the idea into the child's head and that the child's account is therefore false.

The court may edit out improper leading questions during the interview or disallow the whole interview

3.55   If leading questions are judged by the court to have been improperly used during the interview it may well be decided not to show the whole or that part of the recording to the court, so that the child's answers will be lost. Alternatively the whole interview may be played, leaving the judge to comment to the jury, where appropriate, on the weight to be given to that part of the evidence which was led. Neither outcome is desirable, and both can be avoided if interviewers keep off leading questions (see also part 3A, paragraph 3.33-3.35).

Previous statements

Courts will not usually allow witnesses to talk about their previous statements or what others said

3.56   A witness in court is likely to be prevented by the court from giving evidence of what he or she has previously said or what was said to him or her by another person. If allowed in evidence, previous statements might have two functions. First, in the case of the witness's own statement, the court might be asked to take account of the fact that the witness has consistently said the same thing in deciding whether he or she is to be trusted. Secondly, in the case both of the witness's own statements and of statements made to him or her by others, the court might be asked to take the further step of deciding that what was said out of court was true. In a criminal trial, both functions are frowned upon: the first because, in law, it says little for the reliability of a witness to show that he or she has been consistent, and the second because courts are reluctant to accept statements as true unless made in court and subject to the test of cross-examination.

Previous statements showing consistency

But there are exceptions to the previous statements rule

3.57   Although consistency adds little to the credibility of the witness, it will always be proper for the interviewer to ask the child if he or she has told anyone about the alleged incident(s), who he or she told, when he or she told them, and why. But the interview must not ask the child *details* of what was said except in certain circumstances. These circumstances are as follows:

> (a) when a child has *voluntarily given details of an alleged sexual offence soon after that offence took place.* A complaint of buggery made by a boy six months after the incident upon being forcefully questioned by his mother would not be admissible, but the details of a spontaneous allegation of buggery made by the boy on the day of the incident could be mentioned.

> (b) when a child has previously made a *positive identification of the accused.* Identification may be formal (in the course of an identification parade) or informal, for example where a child points out the accused to a teacher and says 'This man tried to push me into his car.' Where such a prior identification has been made, it may be referred to in the video recorded interview.

> The only case which may give rise to difficulty is where there is some doubt as to the fairness of the identification. If, for example, a child tells her father that she has just been sexually assaulted by a man in a leather jacket, and the father apprehends the first leather-clad man that he sees and demands 'Is this him?', a court might be understandably reluctant to admit the child's positive answer as a positive identification and it should not therefore be mentioned in the video recorded interview. The interviewer must therefore be aware of the circumstances of any identification made by the child before the interview.

Previous statements showing truth

Hearsay is not normally allowed

3.58   The technical name for an out-of-court statement which is used in court to prove that what was said is true is *'hearsay'*. The general rule is that hearsay is inadmissible in a criminal trial. In one famous case a little girl who was adjudged too young to give evidence told her mother that she had been indecently assaulted by a 'coloured boy'. A white man was charged but he could not call the mother to give evidence of what the child had said because the child's statement had been made out of court and was hearsay. The same result would have followed if the child had said that her attacker was white and the prosecution had wished to refer to her statement.

3.59   Words (and conduct eg nodding in agreement) are only hearsay if used to prove their truth. There may be other reasons for proving that words were spoken in which case the hearsay rule is not broken. For example a witnesses' report of a child's statement 'Dad taught me to fuck' would be admissible to demonstrate a child's use of age-inappropriate language but inadmissible as evidence that the child's father had had intercourse with her.

But there are exceptions to the hearsay rule

3.60 As with most other rules of evidence, the hearsay rule is not absolute. The use of a video recording of an interview with a child as part of the child's evidence is itself an example of a statutory exception to the rule. Without a detailed appreciation of the scope of the exceptions it will be difficult for an interviewer to gauge the chances of a hearsay statement being regarded as admissible in court and it is best to aim to avoid the inclusion of previous statements in the interview so far as possible. There are a couple of rules of thumb which should assist:

Don't ask the child to talk about what he or she or others said about the alleged offence

(a) Any statements made by the child about the alleged offence prior to the interview are likely to be hearsay. Therefore, subject to the advice in paragraph 3.57, such statements should not be deliberately elicited from the child during a video recorded interview. For example a child should not be asked to relate any conversations he or she may have had concerning the offence.

If you have to accept hearsay for the sake of the interview, try to recapture non-hearsay information later

If the child spontaneously begins an account of what has been said to him or her the interviewer may decide that it is best not to interrupt. If so it should be remembered that this section of the tape is likely to be edited so it will be necessary to go over any relevant non-hearsay information gleaned at this point at a later stage of the interview.

Don't try to describe non-verbal responses yourself

(b) The video recording should capture the child's responses directly as the interviewer's description of the child's response is itself hearsay. For example, if a child is asked where she was touched by an abuser and in response she points to her genitals, that action should be captured by the camera. It will not be enough for the interviewer to say 'She is pointing to her genitals' as this is a statement of the interviewer, not the child. Once this is understood it should be relatively easy to ensure that the relevant evidence comes from the child.

Character of the accused

The courts will not normally allow references to the accused's criminal record or bad reputation

3.61 An important rule of evidence concerns the previous bad character of the accused. Under this rule it is not generally permissible for the prosecution to bring evidence of the accused's bad record or reputation, or of other misconduct in which he or she has been involved, in order simply to show the court that he or she is a bad person who is likely to do wrong. For example, a jury trying a man for sexual offences against a child is likely to be kept in ignorance of his criminal record for such offences or of other charges of a similar nature which may have been made against him. The interviewer must be very careful to avoid mention of such matters and should try to steer the child away from any mention of such discreditable facts.

An exception the rule against evidence of bad character might be made for certain cases of multipe abuse

3.62 The rule against admitting evidence showing the accused's bad character is, like the hearsay rule, subject to exception. Evidence of one offence may be admissible in the case of another offence by reason of the close connection or similarity between them. For example, where two or more children claim to have been indecently assaulted by the same person the evidence of one child is sometimes used to support the allegations of the other. This is only permissible where the evidence goes beyond showing that the accused is a 'bad person likely to do wrong' and independently suggests that he is the person who committed the offence or offences in question. In other words, the probative value of the evidence must outweigh its prejudicial effect.

Two recordings should be considered in multiple abuse cases

3.63 In many cases the line between admissibility and inadmissibility is a difficult one to draw. Complex legal considerations are involved. All that can be done before the trial is to estimate the chances that the court will be prepared, say, to hear that a school-teacher has been accused of buggery by four of his pupils, or a father of incest by two daughters. This presents no difficulty for the interviewer if the evidence of one child is quite separate from that of another. But it may be that the victim of one offence claims to have witnessed the occurrence of another offence against a different victim. In such cases it might be advisable, following consultation with the Crown Prosecution Service, to record separately the child's account of (i) offences allegedly committed against him or her, and (ii) what he or she knows about offences involving other victims.

Court's discretion to exclude evidence

Courts can exclude evidence if it is unfair even if it doesn't breach the strict rules of evidence

3.64   A court trying a criminal case has the power to exclude evidence tendered on behalf of the prosecution, even though the evidence complies with the strict rules of admissibility. Under section 78 of the Police and Criminal Evidence Act 1984, the court may exclude evidence on the grounds that, because of the way in which it was obtained or for any other reason, the admission of the evidence would have such an adverse effect on the fairness of the proceedings that the court ought not to admit it. Courts may also exercise a common law power (that is, one supported by previous decisions of the courts) to exclude evidence the prejudicial effect of which outweighs its probative value. The definition of these powers is deliberately broad in order to preserve their flexibility. Interviewers can guard against their exercise by following the provisions of this Memorandum and by taking any other steps which appear to them to be necessary to ensure that no unfairness ensues from their procedures.

PART 4

AFTER THE INTERVIEW

4.1   This part of the Memorandum gives advice about the storage, custody and destruction of the video recording and about its viewing by others, including for training purposes.

The video recording must be kept strictly confidential

4.2   A video recording made in accordance with this Memorandum is likely to be a highly valuable piece of evidence. It may well also contain intimate, personal information and images and, in the child's interests, should be held strictly in confidence and for its proper purpose. It is therefore essential that adequate arrangements are made to store the recording safely and securely and to ensure that access to it, and to any copies which are made, is restricted to those who are authorised to view the recording.

Ownership

4.3   The video recording will be treated as a *document*[1] for the purposes of criminal proceedings and the statements in it will not belong to anybody except insofar as they are the property of the persons who made them. However, the medium on which the statements are made is likely to be the property of the police or social services (as the case may be) and the fact of ownership of the videotape itself conveys certain rights and responsibilities which, if properly exercised, will help ensure that the recording is appropriately safeguarded.

The Video should be treated as a police exhibit

4.4   It is recommended that *all* videotapes containing interviews prepared under the joint police/social services or NSPCC investigation arrangements set out in this Memorandum should be treated as exhibits and maintained for these purposes by the police. But choices about access to them should be taken jointly by the agencies involved in their preparation. Once the case has been passed to the Crown Prosecution Service, decisions as to disclosure of information will be made by them. In taking such decisions, all agencies should have regard to the provisions in paragraphs 4.11 to 4.17 (see also annex J).

Registration

Record interview details in a log book

4.5   The details of all video recorded interviews should be carefully registered in a log book kept for the purpose by the police. The log book should record the number of the recording, the venue of the interview, the names of the child and of the interviewer (and all others present) and the date and time of the interview(s).

Before storage

Rewind tape and protect from erasure

4.6   Once the recording is finished, the tape should be carefully rewound and ejected from the recorder. The "record protect" device fitted to cassettes should be activated to prevent accidental erasure of the recording.

Check tape and prepare a written index

4.7   The tape should be checked for the quality of the recording *and it is recommended that a brief index to the tape is prepared at this stage, in*

---

[1]See annex A

31

liaison with the interviewer, so that the most relevant passages regarding the alleged offence can be readily located later on. A specimen index sheet is at annex K. The index is not a full transcript or précis of the tape but it should serve similar purposes, enhanced by the video recording itself. The index should be carefully preserved and safeguarded along with the other papers on the case. If a summary of the interview has also been prepared a copy should be kept with the index.

Carefully label all tapes

4.8   The master tape of the video recording and all copies should be individually labelled and registered in the log book so that the copies can be distinguished from one another and so that the master tape can be readily identified. The ownership of the master tape should be treated in the same way as an exhibit for use in court and a signed exhibit label should be placed over the open side of its box. The seal should not be broken except in the presence of a representative of the Crown Prosecution Service and for the reasons set out in paragraphs 4.11 to 4.13. The ownership of the master tape and any copy should be clearly marked and with a warning that none must be copied, or shown to unauthorised persons. A recommended form of words for the label is set out at annex L.

Storage

Store tapes securely

4.9   The tapes should be placed in boxes, preferably of a type which incorporate a device for preventing rotation of the hubs.

4.10   The tapes should always be kept in locked, secure containers. They should never be left lying about so that unauthorised persons can gain access to them. Videotapes should not be subjected to extremes of temperature or humidity (for this latter reason they should not be sealed in air-tight containers) and they should be stored away from electrical or magnetic fields, for example away from electric motors or loudspeakers.

Copies and access

4.11   Decisions about copying and allowing access to video recordings prepared under this Memorandum should be taken individually and with careful regard to the following principles:

Copying and access must be kept to the minimum

A   Copying of and access to the video or audio tape of the interview should be confined to the absolute minimum consistent with the interests of the child and the interests of justice.

Don't lend a copy to anyone who might not look after it properly

B   No one should have custody of any such tape unless he or she is able and willing to safeguard it to the standard recommended by this Memorandum.

Never let a copy get into the hands of the accused

C   No person accused or implicated in relation to the alleged offences should himself or herself have custody or unsupervised access to that tape.

The investigating team and the CPS may need a copy...

...and so might the defence (but not the defendant)

Get a written undertaking as in annex J

4.12   In most criminal cases the joint investigating team and the Crown Prosecution Service will need access to a recording and so will the court. A further copy will also be required if one needs to be disclosed to the defendant's legal representative because it is part, or all, of the case against the accused. Where a defendant is unrepresented, access should be under strict police supervision. Any access should be authorized only in respect of named individuals. If such individuals wish to borrow the tape they must be able to give a written undertaking about the protection he or she will provide to the tape whilst it is in his or her custody and must confirm that it will be returned to the police at the end of the proceedings. A form of undertaking, based on a model developed by the Law Society, is at annex J.

Don't accept applications to view or borrow at face value...

...and try to arrange access rather than loan if possible

Warn about criminal penalities for misuse or unauthorised retention

Log all loans and access...

Don't erase a recording without joint consultation

Seek consent before using tapes for training

4.13   Applications to view or borrow a recording from other individuals or agencies should be scrutinised carefully. Claims to be acting in the interests of the child or of justice should be validated and considered on their merits. Consideration should always be given to allowing supervised access in preference to lending a tape; and to loan in preference to making a further copy.

4.14   Any person borrowing the tape should have his or her attention drawn to the ownership of the tape itself; to the likelihood that the recording will form part of a criminal trial; and to the fact that its misuse or unauthorised retention may constitute a contempt of court or other criminal offence.

4.15   Details of the movements of any tape and, on each occasion, the name(s) of persons allowed to view or borrow a recording, together with details of the specific authority granted to them should always be carefully recorded in the police log book (see paragraph 4.5 above). Log books for this purpose should also be maintained by any body authorised to have custody of a copy, and such log books should be subject to such periodic inspection by management as may be required.

Destruction of tapes

4.16   Video recordings should be destroyed when it is clear that their continued existence serves no further purpose. Since a recording would be likely to be needed for any appeal proceedings it will be necessary to store the master copy for a considerable number of years. A decision to erase a video recording should be taken jointly by a nominated senior police officer and a nominated senior Social Services manager. The decision and the reasons for it should be recorded in the log book referred to at paragraph 4.5. Care should be taken to ensure that erasure is complete, including all of the soundtrack.

Use of tapes for training

4.17   Video recorded interviews should not be used for training or other purposes unless specific and informed consent has been given for that purpose, preferably by the child himself or herself. Alternatively, if the child is unable to understand the concept, the adult who discharges the principal duty of care for the child should be consulted. But every effort should be made to discuss the matter with the child and in a way the child can understand. The child should be reassured that granting consent at this stage does not mean that anyone who wishes to see the video will be able to do so. Consent should not be sought before the interview, nor will it always be right to do so immediately afterwards. If consent is granted, this fact should be recorded in the log book.

Admissible evidence (statements including videos) – Oral statements made in court concerning facts directly experienced by the speaker plus certain narrow exceptions defined by rules established by the courts and by statute law. Under the Criminal Justice Act 1988 (as amended) a video recording of an interview with a child can be admissible evidence even though it may break the normal rules. But once the video has been allowed into court the normal rules on admissibility may be applied to the evidence it contains. *See also Part 3B of this Memorandum.*

Burden of proof – In proceedings for a criminal offence the defendant is generally presumed to be innocent. This means that in order for the court to convict him, the prosecution must carry the burden of proving that the defendant committed the offence alleged, and must do so beyond reasonable doubt. In civil proceedings it is generally for the party bringing the proceedings to prove its case on the balance of probabilities.

Child – There are several definitions of "child" for legal purposes. For the purposes of this Memorandum, a child is a person aged under 14 who has witnessed or been the victim of a violent offence, or one under 17 in the case of a sexual offence. *A chart summarising the age limits which apply at the various stages in the criminal process from the point where the video recording is made, is at the end of this annex.*

Civil Proceedings – A case at civil law is normally one between private persons and/or private organisations. Typically it will be about defining the rights and relations between individuals (for example, matrimonial proceedings and disputes about who should have the custody of a child).

Committal for trial – Normally persons charged with an offence come before a **magistrates' court** for a preliminary hearing. The magistrates' court will commit the defendant to the **Crown Court** for trial when (i) the offence is very serious and may only be tried in the Crown Court (ie it is "triable only on **indictment**"); or (ii) the offence may be tried either in the Crown Court or the magistrates' court, and either the magistrates' court decides that it is too serious for them to try or the defendant himself elects trial by jury in the Crown Court. Under Section 53 of the Criminal Justice Act 1991, the Director of Public Prosecutions can issue a notice which has the effect of bypassing the magistrates' court **committal proceedings** altogether where there is a child witness and the alleged offence was one of the violent and sexual offences specified in the Act and where the Crown Court could try the case.

Committal proceedings – Where the magistrates examine the prosecution evidence to check that there is enough to justify a trial. In recent years the magistrates have usually done this by considering the written statements in the case but it remains possible for the defendant to insist on the prosecution's witnesses giving their evidence orally and in person (the so-called "old-style committal").

Compellability – The general rule is that if a witness is **competent** to give evidence they are also compellable. That means the court can insist on them giving evidence. The attendance of a witness can be compelled, for example, in the **Crown Court** by means of a witness summons or order, the failure to comply with which is a contempt of court. There are exceptions to the general rule that all competent witnesses are compellable. Witnesses who are competent but not compellable for either side include the Sovereign, foreign sovereigns and those entitled to claim diplomatic privilege. For the defence the co-accused is not compellable for the other(s). Spouses are only compellable for the defence (again, unless they are co-accused); they are only compellable for the prosecution in respect of assaults on the spouse or a child under 16, or a sexual offence against a child under 16.

Competence (of witness) – In criminal proceedings a witness may give evidence only if he or she is competent. A witness is competent if he or she is capable of telling the truth and of giving rational testimony. It is for the trial judge to decide if a particular witness is incapable of meeting the criteria of competency. Competence requirements do not apply at all in some civil proceedings; in others a different requirement may apply. Neither the accused nor any co-accused is competent for the prosecution. The Criminal Justice Act 1991 reforms the special rules about the competency of child witnesses – *see Part 2, paragraph 2.13 of this Memorandum.*

Cross-examination – The procedure in the trial **after examination in chief** where the lawyer representing the side which did not call the witness seeks to establish its own case by questioning the other side's witness. Section 32A of the Criminal Justice Act 1988 makes it a condition of accepting the video that the child is available for cross-examination but it ensures that the child witness can be cross-examined from outside the courtroom via a **live television link**. Furthermore, Section 34A of the Criminal Justice Act 1988 (as added by the 1991 Act) forbids cross-examination of the child by the accused in person.

Crown Court – The criminal court that tries those charged with offences which are generally too serious for the magistrates' court to deal with. This includes the most serious offences which are triable only on **indictment** such as rape. The Crown Court may impose any sentence up to the maximum permitted by law for the offence, or a fine of any amount. The Crown Court also hears appeals against convictions or sentences imposed in the **magistrates' courts**. At present **live television link** facilities are available only in the Crown Court.

Document – The Civil Evidence Act 1968 defines "document" to include "any disc, tape, sound track or any other device in which sounds or other data (not being visual images) are embodied so as to be capable (with or without the aid of some other equipment) of being reproduced therefrom"; and "any film, negative, tape or other device in which one or more visual images are embodied so as to be capable (as aforesaid) of being reproduced therefrom." This definition of document is incorporated into the Criminal Justice Act 1988 by Schedule 2, paragraph 5.

Evidence in chief – The evidence which a witness gives in response to examination on behalf of the party who has brought the person forward as a witness (see **examination in chief**). Once evidence in chief has been completed, the witness is made available for **cross-examination** by the other party or parties to the proceedings.

Examination in chief – The procedure in the trial where, normally, the lawyer representing the side who has called the witness takes that person through his or her evidence (see **evidence in chief**). The Criminal Justice Act 1988 (as amended) allows a video recording of an earlier interview with the child to be played instead. Depending on the matters raised in **cross-examination**, the party who called the witness in the first place may choose to conduct a further examination in chief, or re-examination, as it is called. Thus, for example, where the prosecution calls a woman to give evidence that she has been raped by two men, she will give evidence in chief on behalf of the prosecution, and will be open to cross-examination on behalf of both defendants, with the prosecution having the option to re-examine.

Indictment – A bill of indictment is a written or printed accusation of crime made usually at the suit of the Crown against one or more persons. This is the method by which the most serious offences are tried, known as "indictable offences".

Interests of justice – Those interests which, according to section 32A of the Criminal Justice Act 1988 (as added by the 1991 Act), must be shown to be in jeopardy before the court can agree to exclude an otherwise acceptable video recording. The 1988 Act does not define "interests of justice"; it is for the court to determine in the light of all the circumstances. It will be for the party objecting to the use in evidence of the recording to show the court why it should exercise this power. If the recording contains a clear account by the child of matters which clearly relate to the trial, then, provided always that the other statutory conditions are satisfied, the court is unlikely to reject the whole of the recording unless it considers that to use it would be in some way prejudicial to the accused person (or, if there is more than one, to anyone who stands accused.) If only part of the recording is objected to, the statute expressly states that the court must weigh any prejudice to an accused which might result from showing that part of the recording against the desirability of showing the whole, or substantially the whole, of it.

Live television links – The Criminal Justice Act 1988 enabled evidence from children under 14 years of age to be given via a live television link in cases involving certain violent and sexual offences. This system spares child witnesses from the ordeal of appearing in open court in the presence of the alleged abuser while preserving the right of the defence to question the child and giving the jury the opportunity to observe the child's demeanour while he or she is being **cross-examined**. It is for the judge to decide whether a child witness may give evidence in this way but it is very rare for an application to be rejected.

The child sits in front of a television monitor in a room adjacent to the courtroom, accompanied by an usher or other adult supporter. The child will see on the screen the faces of the judge and counsel in turn as they question him or her. The judge, counsel and the jury can see the child's face on the television monitors in the courtroom. In addition the judge sees on his monitor not only the child but also, from a second camera, the room in which the child is sitting and thus any accompanying person. This latter image is inset into the corner of the screen on the judge's monitor.

The 1988 Act provisions were extended by the 1991 Act so that they are now available to any young person who is to be cross-examined at the trial following the admission of video recorded evidence.

Magistrates' court – A court of summary jurisdiction in which all criminal cases normally commence. Some cases will be committed to the **Crown Court** for trial or sentence; those offences which are triable summarily only are tried in a magistrates' court.

Video recording – According to section 34A of the Criminal Justice Act 1988 (as added by the Criminal Justice Act 1991) "video recording" means "any recording, on any medium, from which a moving image may by any means be produced and includes the accompanying sound track". *See also* **Document**.

Youth court – In criminal cases, this court name replaces the old "juvenile court". Under the 1991 Act it will deal with criminal cases where the defendant is aged under 18. Like the juvenile court, it will remain a branch of the **magistrates' court**.

AGE LIMITS –
THE SIX CATEGORIES

	Violent Offences	Sexual Offences	Reference
Making the Video	U14	U17	Section 32A(7)[1] Criminal Justice Act 1988
Transfer	U14, or U15 if U14 when video made	U17, or U18 if U17 when video made	Section 53 CJA 1991
Deciding whether to admit video in evidence	U14, or U15 if U14 when video made	U17, or U18 if U17 when video made	Section 32A(7)[1] CJA 1988
Eligibility for live TV links	U14, or pursuant to video	U17, or pursuant to video	Section 32(1)(b)[1] CJA 1988
Protected from cross-examination by accused	U14, or pursuant to video	U17, or pursuant to video	Section 34A(2)[1] CJA 1988
Protected from giving live evidence at committal proceedings	U14, or U15 if U14 when video made	U17, or U18 if U17 when video made	Section 55(1) and Section 53(6) CJA 1991

---

[1]as amended by the Criminal Justice Act 1991.

32A. (1)   This section applies in relation to the following proceedings, namely-

>   (a)   trials on indictment for any offence to which section 32(2) above applies;

>   (b)   appeals to the criminal division of the Court of Appeal and hearings of references under section 17 of the Criminal Appeal Act 1968 in respect of any such offence; and

>   (c)   proceedings in youth courts for any such offence and appeals to the Crown Court arising out of such proceedings.

(2)   In any such proceedings a video recording of an interview which-

>   (a)   is conducted between an adult and a child who is not the accused or one of the accused ("the child witness"); and

>   (b)   relates to any matter in issue in the proceedings, may, with the leave of the court, be given in evidence in so far as it is not excluded by the court under subsection (3) below.

(3)   Where a video recording is tendered in evidence under this section, the court shall (subject to the exercise of any power of the court to exclude evidence which is otherwise admissible) give leave under subsection (2) above unless-

>   (a)   it appears that the child witness will not be available for cross-examination;

>   (b)   any rules of court requiring disclosure of the circumstances in which the video was made have not been complied with to the satisfaction of the court; or

>   (c)   the court is of the opinion, having regard to all the circumstances of the case, that in the interests of justice the recording ought not to be admitted; and where the court gives such leave it may, if it is of the opinion that in the interests of justice any part of the recording ought not to be admitted, direct that that part shall be excluded.

(4)   In considering whether any part of a recording ought to be excluded under subsection (3) above, the court shall consider whether any prejudice to the accused, or one of the accused, which might result from the admission of that part is outweighed by the desirability of showing the whole, or substantially the whole, of the recorded interview.

(5)   Where a video recording is admitted under this section-

>   (a)   the child witness shall be called by the party who tendered it in evidence;

>   (b)   that witness shall not be examined in chief on any matter which, in the opinion of the court, has been dealt with in his recorded testimony.

(6)   Where a video recording is given in evidence under this section, any statement made by the child witness which is disclosed by the recording shall be treated as if given by that witness in direct oral testimony; and accordingly-

>   (a)   any such statement shall be admissible evidence of any fact of which such testimony from him would be admissible;

38

(b)   no such statement shall be capable of corroborating any other evidence given by him; and in estimating the weight, if any, to be attached to such a statement, regard shall be had to all the circumstances from which any inference can reasonably be drawn (as to its accuracy or otherwise).

(7)   In this section "child" means a person who-

(a)   in the case of an offence falling within section 32(2)(a) or (b) above, is under fourteen years of age or, if he was under that age when the video recording was made, is under fifteen years of age; or

(b)   in the case of an offence falling within section 32(2)(c) above, is under seventeen years of age or, if he was under that age when the video recording was made, is under eighteen years of age.

(8)   Any reference in subsection (7) above to an offence falling within paragraph (a), (b) or (c) of section 32(2) above includes a reference to an offence which consists of attempting or conspiring to commit, or of aiding, abetting, counselling, procuring or inciting the commission of, an offence falling within that paragraph.

(9)   In this section-

"statement" includes any representation of fact, whether made in words or otherwise;

"video recording" means any recording, on any medium, from which a moving image may by any means be produced and includes the accompanying sound-track.

(10)   A magistrates' court inquiring into an offence as examining justices under section 6 of the Magistrates' Courts Act 1980 may consider any video recording as respects which leave under subsection (2) above is to be sought at the trial, notwithstanding that the child witness is not called at the committal proceedings.

(11)   Without prejudice to the generality of any enactment conferring power to make rules of court, such rules may make such provision as appears to the authority making them to be necessary or expedient for the purposes of this section.

(12)   Nothing in this section shall prejudice the admissibility of any video recording which would be admissible apart from this section.

Sexual Offences Act 1956

Rape	s.1
Procurement of woman by threats	s.2
Procurement of woman by false pretences	s.3
Administering drugs to obtain or facilitate intercourse	s.4
Intercourse with girl under thirteen	s.5
Intercourse with girl under sixteen	s.6
Intercourse with defective	s.7
Procurement of defective	s.9
Incest by a man	s.10
Incest by a woman	s.11
Buggery	s.12
Indecency between men	s.13
Indecent assault on a woman	s.14
Indecent assault on a man	s.15
Assault with intent to commit buggery	s.16
Abduction of woman by force or for the sake of her property	s.17
Abduction of girl under eighteen from parent or guardian	s.19
Abduction of girl under sixteen from parent or guardian	s.20
Abduction of defective from parent or guardian	s.21
Causing prostitution of a woman	s.22
Procuration of girl under twenty-one	s.23
Detention of woman in brothel	s.24
Permitting girl under thirteen to use premises for intercourse	s.25
Permitting girl under sixteen to use premises for intercourse	s.26
Permitting defective to use premises for intercourse	s.27
Causing or encouraging prostitution etc of girl under sixteen	s.28
Causing or encouraging prostitution of defective	s.29
Living on earnings of prostitution	s.30
Controlling a prostitute	s.31
Solicitation by a man	s.32
Keeping a brothel	s.33
Letting premises for use as brothel	s.34
Tenant permitting premises to be used as brothel	s.35
Tenant permitting premises to be used for prostitution	s.36

Indecency with Children Act 1960

Indecency with a child	s.1

Sexual Offences Act 1967

Living on earnings of male prostitution	s.5

Criminal Law Act 1977

Incitement to commit incest	s.54

Protection of Children Act 1978

Indecent photographs of children	s.1

LEGAL ELEMENTS OF MAIN SEXUAL AND VIOLENT OFFENCES

The contents of this Annex should not be taken as a complete statement of all the relevant legal provisions. If in doubt obtain legal advice.

OFFENCE	WHAT NEEDS TO BE ESTABLISHED
Sexual intercourse and buggery	
Rape Section 1, Sexual Offences Act 1956	a) Sexual intercourse ie penetration of the vagina by the penis (however slight), not necessarily resulting in emission b) the woman[1] did not consent. (Where the victim is a very young child, her age may be enough to show that she did not (or could not) consent. But generally there should be evidence of lack of consent, such as resistence.) c) the man knew this, or was reckless as to whether she consented
Buggery Section 12, Sexual Offences Act 1956	If with woman, <u>male under 21</u>, or child under 16 a) Penetration of anus by penis occurred If with male over 21 (and defendant is male over 21) a) Penetration of anus by penis occurred b) act was either not in private, involved more than two men, or was non-consensual. If with <u>animal</u> any act of sexual intercourse with the animal NB: Whether the person consented will generally be relevant in sentencing.
Intercourse with girl under 13 Section 5, Sexual Offences Act 1956	a) Sexual intercourse (see notes on rape and incest for definition) occurred with a girl under 13 NB: The girl's consent is irrelevant, although if the girl did not consent, rape may be charged – see above

[1]Any reference to "woman" or "man" includes "girl" or "boy" (as the case may be) unless otherwise indicated in the text.

OFFENCE	WHAT NEEDS TO BE ESTABLISHED
Intercourse with girl under 16 Section 6, Sexual Offences Act 1956	a) Sexual intercourse occurred with girl under 16 Defences: a) Defendant under 24 who has not been charged with this offence before has a defence if he believed, with reasonable cause, that the girl was 16 or over b) intercourse occurred as a result of a marriage and the defendant believed, with reasonable cause, that the girl was his wife (notwithstanding that the marriage was invalid because of the girl's age) NB: Same considerations apply concerning consent as above
Incest by a man Section 10, Sexual Offences Act 1956	a) Sexual intercourse (penetration of vagina by penis) occurred b) that the defendant knew the person was his grand-daughter, daughter, sister or mother (includes half-sisters etc) NB: The relationships need not be traced through lawful wedlock
Incest by a woman Section 11, Sexual Offences Act 1956	a) Woman of 16 consented to sexual intercourse b) she knew the person was her grand-father, father, brother or son (includes half-brothers etc) NB: As above
Incitement to commit incest Section 54, Sexual Offences Act 1956	a) That man incited a woman to have sexual intercourse with him b) that the woman was his grand-daughter, daughter or sister (includes half-sisters etc.) c) that the man knows that she is such
Permitting girl under 13 to use premises for sexual intercourse Section 25, Sexual Offences Act 1956	a) Defendant was owner or occupier of the premises, or acts or assists in their management b) defendant either induced or allowed a girl under 13 to use premises for sexual intercourse
Permitting girl under 16 to use premises for sexual intercourse Section 25, Sexual Offences Act 1956	a) Defendant was owner or occupier of the premises, or acts or assists in their management b) defendant either induced or allowed a girl under 16 to use premises for sexual intercourse
Assault with intent to commit buggery Section 16, Sexual Offences Act 1956	a) That an assault has occured b) The purpose of the assault was to facilitate an act of buggery (see above for definition of buggery)

OFFENCE	WHAT NEEDS TO BE ESTABLISHED
Administering drugs to obtain or facilitate intercourse Section 4, Sexual Offences Act 1956	a) Defendant caused woman to take any drug, matter or thing (i.e. without her knowledge or consent) b) with intent to overpower or stupefy her c) that the purpose of this is to enable any man, whether the defendant or another, to have sexual intercourse with her
Indecency	
Indecent assault on a woman Section 14, Sexual Offences Act 1956	a) That an assault occurred (any physical contact is sufficient) b) it has a sexual nature c) it is either inherently indecent, or it is capable of being indecent and is accompanied by an indecent motive NB: A girl under 16 or a defective can give no consent which would negate the assault
Indecent assault on a man Section 15, Sexual Offences Act 1956	a) That an assault occurred b) it is indecent, or at least capable of being indecent and is accompanied by an indecent motive NB: A boy under 16, or a defective can give no consent which would negate the assault
Indecency with a child Section 1, Indecency with Children Act 1960	a) Defendant committed a grossly indecent act with or towards a child under 14 (jury to decide what is grossly indecent, but covers activities such as genital touching etc; an act such as masturbation may be covered if it is done towards a child, i.e. where the defendant derives sexual pleasure from the child's presence); or b) defendant incited a child under 14 to commit such an act with him or another
Indecency between men (See also **Indecency with Children,** below) Section 13, Sexual Offences Act 1956	a) Participation of both men b) that a grossly indecent act occurred (the term is not defined but covers mutual masturbation etc.) NB: No offence is committed if both the parties are over 21 and the act occurs in private. Procuring or attempting to procure a grossly indecent act does not necessarily require the willing participation of both men
Indecent photographs of children Section 1, Protection of Children Act 1978	a) That defendant either took, or allowed to be taken; showed; distributed; possessed with a view to distributing or showing; or advertised, a photograph of any child under 16, and b) that said photograph is indecent c) where taking an indecent photograph of a child is alleged, that the defendant deliberately and intentionally took such a photograph

OFFENCE	WHAT NEEDS TO BE ESTABLISHED
Prostitution etc	
Causing prostitution of a woman Section 22, Sexual Offences Act 1956	a) Woman was procured to become a common prostitute (a woman who offers her body to all and sundry for acts of a sexual nature, for payment) b) that woman was procured to leave her normal address in the UK to frequent a brothel elsewhere NB: This offence must be supported by corroborating evidence

Causing or encouraging prostitution of girl under 16
 	
Section 28, Sexual Offences Act 1956
	a) Defendant has responsibility for the girl
	
	b) defendant causes, or encourages either:
	    (i) prostitution of girl
	    (ii) unlawful sexual intercourse involving the girl
	    (iii) any indecent act involving the girl
	
	NB: Where the girl has either become a prostitute, had sexual intercourse or taken part in indecent acts, and the defendant allowed her to consort with any prostitute or other person of known immoral character, then the defendant is deemed guilty of causing the girl's behaviour.

Solicitation by a man Section 32, Sexual Offences Act 1956	a) Defendant committed more than one act of importuning b) that the importuning was for an immoral purpose (question for the jury to decide according to contemporary standards of moral behaviour)
Abduction	
Abduction of girl under 18 from her parent or guardian Section 19, Sexual Offences Act 1956	a) Defendant took girl from her guardian(s) without consent; or the defendant persuaded the girl to leave her guardian b) the intent behind the taking was for the girl to have sexual intercourse, whether with the defendant or any other Defence: The defendant has reasonable cause to believe the girl is over 18
Abduction of girl under 16 from parent or guardian Section 20, Sexual Offences Act 1956	a) Defendant took girl out of possession of guardian(s) against their will, or defendant persuaded her to leave

OFFENCE	WHAT NEEDS TO BE ESTABLISHED
Violence and cruelty	

Cruelty to children
 	
Section 1, Children and Young Persons Act 1933
	a) Defendant has attained age of 16
	
	b) Defendant has responsibility for person below 16
	
	c) Defendant either:
	
	    (i) assaults;
	    (ii) ill-treats;
	    (iii) abandons; or
	    (iv) exposes
	
	the child or causes or procures any of these so that the child suffers unnecessarily or his health is damaged

Assault Common law	Defendant deliberately made physical contact or intentionally or recklessly caused another to fear or apprehend immediate violence
Assault occasioning actual bodily harm Section 47, Offences Against the Person Act 1861	a) Defendant assaulted person b) assault caused hurt or injury calculated to interfere with the health or comfort of another

Grievous Bodily harm or Wounding
 	
Section 20, Offences Against the Person Act 1861
	a) Defendant either:
	
	    (i) causes or inflicts serious bodily harm such as broken bones etc; or
	    (ii) breaks the victim's skin
	
	b) Defendant intended to cause physical harm, or foresaw that any such harm might be caused

Grievous bodily harm, or wounding with intent
 	
Section 18, Offences Against the Person Act 1861
	a) Defendant either:
	
	    (i) causes or inflicts serious bodily harm such as broken bones etc; or
	    (ii) breaks the victim's skin
	
	b) Defendant must have intended serious bodily harm

OFFENCE	WHAT NEEDS TO BE ESTABLISHED
Manslaughter Common law	a) Defendant killed victim and at least one of the following applies – b) (i) death due to defendant's recklessness; or (ii) death due to gross negligence on part of defendant; or (iii) death result of an unlawful act on part of the defendant, which he should have realised carried a risk of some harm; or (iv) defendant's mental responsibility was diminished at the time of act; or (v) defendant suddenly and temporarily lost self-control because of a provoking event; or (vi) death was in pursuance of a suicide pact
Murder Common law	a) Defendant killed victim b) that he did so either intentionally or as a result of intending to cause grievous bodily harm
Attempts to commit any of the above	In general: a) the intention required for the complete offence b) acts by the defendant which are more than merely preparatory

The Crown Court (Amendment) Rules 1992 and The Criminal Justice Act 1991 (Dismissal of Transferred Charges) Rules 1992 are available from HMSO.

Preliminaries

F1.   The following guidance sets out basic recommendations about the type of equipment that should achieve a standard of recording which is adequate for use in court and likely to meet the requirements of the court rules. *Basic hand-held equipment cannot generally be relied upon to reach the required standard* and should only be used in exceptional circumstances, for example when a child is hospitalised.

F2.   Whatever equipment is chosen should be within the competency of the operator, properly maintained, and regularly tested prior to each interview. Such testing should involve making a short recording using sound and vision and replaying the recording on another machine to confirm that the quality is adequate. Testing should be the responsibility of a local technician or suitably trained person.

F3.   The interview room should be selected to ensure a reasonably quiet location away from noisy traffic or other sources of local noise such as offices, toilets, banging doors etc. It should have a carpeted floor and curtains on the windows. Ideally it should be a rectangular room (not square) and no larger than necessary (less than 5m by 4m). When furnishing the room for the interview, consideration should be given to avoiding a loud and cluttered image on the screen. The furniture should be set out in advance in relation to camera angles and light source (see below) and, once a suitable arrangement has been established, it might be helpful to mark the position of the furniture on the floor for future reference.

F4.   *It is very important to ensure that neither the furniture, cushions, toys or 'props' are noisy* – the type of children's furniture filled with polystyrene chips is emphatically not recommended and great care should be taken to avoid intrusive noise from any other source, for example from rustling papers.

Vision

F5.   For the purposes of this Memorandum interviews may be carried out using one or two cameras. However, whilst the use of a single fixed camera need not produce a recording of an inferior quality, it will provide less reassurance to the courts as to the conduct of the interview. Rule 23C of the Crown Court (Amendment) Rules 1992 requires the person applying for a video recorded interview to be admitted as part of the child's evidence to provide information to the court of who was present in the room throughout the interview. This requirement can most easily be satisfied by the use of two cameras: one focused on the child and the other giving a good general view of the room. If only one camera is to be used the requirement of the Rules may need to be satisfied by evidence from those who were present at the interview. A single camera system might also be found unsuitable for use where the child is very young or otherwise likely to move around the room.

F6.   If a two camera system is adopted, a vision mixing unit will also be needed to allow the image from the camera recording the whole room to be inset within a corner of the screen, relaying the image from the camera focused on the child. Mounting the cameras close together may avoid a disorienting effect when the images are displayed together on the screen. The exact placement can best be determined by factors such as the location of the doors and windows.

F7.   As far as is technically feasible the *first camera* should aim to show clearly the child's head and face. If this camera is fixed, care should be taken that it is not set too high or so low that the view of the child might be obstructed. A good, clear picture of the child's face may help the court determine what is being said and to assess the emotional state of the child. Every reasonable effort should be made to ensure the definition and quality of the image of the child's face throughout the interview. The *second camera* should give as full a picture as possible of the whole room. The court may need to be reassured that any part of the interview room not recorded by this camera was unoccupied: the placing of fixed furniture in any 'blind spot' could provide that reassurance and should prevent the child from straying into the 'blind area'.

F8.   With careful placing of the furniture in a small room it may be found that the child can be encouraged to settle in a spot and not move far from it during the interview. However some children will prove rather more difficult to constrain. Although this problem might be overcome by zoom and pan/tilt facilities, considerable skill is required in their use. *The operator has no editorial function so far as interpretation of what the child is saying and doing is concerned and must ensure that he or she does not place undue emphasis on particular parts of the child's testimony.*

F9.   A different two camera system to that described above has been found useful in clinical applications dealing with young and disturbed children. The system comprises two colour cameras mounted on the wall diagonally opposite to each other, at eye level. The effective use of such a system is likely to entail specialised, skilled resources and, for criminal proceedings, particular care will be needed to ensure that any decisions about the editing or selection of the camera images are fully consistent with evidential objectives and do not distort or detract from the testimony in any way.

F10.   Modern video equipment does not normally require special additional lighting. Natural daylight may be perfectly adequate, particularly if enhanced by pale coloured walls and a white ceiling. However, shafts of light, or sudden changes in natural light, can present problems for the automatic iris of the camera and should be avoided if possible. If natural daylight proves insufficient or unsuitable, normal fluorescent light can be used effectively. Ideally, the main sources of light should be either side of the camera. A mix of natural light, tungsten and fluorescent light should be avoided. This can cause unnatural effects if colour equipment is used.

Acoustics

F11.   *The evidential value of the video recorded interview will depend very much on the court being able to discern clearly what was said, both by the interviewer and by the child witness.* Provided that a room of the dimensions and furnishings recommended above (see Preliminaries) has been selected, acoustics should not present a problem. *However, the selection and placing of microphones will require very careful attention if a satisfactory recording is to be made.*

F12.   The video recorder should preferably be capable of hi-fi stereo sound recording. At present only ordinary playback facilities are available in Crown Court centres but the enhanced, secure, sound quality available in some cases may be crucial to admissibility and may justify substitution of hi-fi facilities in court. Ideally there should be manual recording level controls for each sound channel so that recording levels can be set appropriate to the facility's needs, together with a sound level meter.

F13.   A microphone of the type normally used for recording interviews with suspects, ie a boundary layer microphone, will also be suitable for the purposes of this Memorandum provided the system is correctly installed. Preferably two microphones should be used with the aim of locating one close to and within two metres of the conversation to provide the main sound recording. A small pre-amplifier should be used with each microphone to bring the signals up to normal audio line input levels.

F14.   Care is also needed in the placing of remote microphones if they are not to obtrude, distract or otherwise impede the child's communication. Some children may find them inhibiting while others may be drawn to them as playthings. A further problem is that some children may move around the room and away from the intended location for which the equipment has been optimally installed. A recommended solution is to mount the second microphone unobtrusively on the wall to provide a second recording which may be used to back up the main recording where the sound has been made less clear due to the movement of the child from the intended location. The use of two microphones will also ensure some sound is recorded if one microphone should fail.

Recorders and tapes

F15.   The format of the equipment should be such as to produce recordings of a suitable quality which can be reproduced in court. The Crown Court centres which are presently used for cases where the child witness is to give evidence via a live television link are supplied with facilities using the VHS format.

F16.   Use of a generator to insert time and date into the picture should avoid the need to demonstrate to the court for each video recording both when the recording was made and the continuity of the interview. Such devices are therefore strongly recommended. Nevertheless, oral statements of the date and time should be made at the beginning and at the close of the interview to confirm that the device is accurate.

F17.   The equipment should ideally be capable of making two simultaneous recordings during the interview: the master copy which should be sealed after the interview (see Part 4 paragraph 4.8), and the working copy. The master should be played only once to check its quality prior to its submission for criminal proceedings. If two recordings are not made during the interview, all copies required must be made in a secure and verifiable way. Whenever possible this should be carried out using police facilities with a statement of where and by whom the copy was made, and confirming that no further copies were made (again, see Part 4 paragraph 4.8).

F18.   Where two recorders are used, the video and audio should not be looped through one recorder to the other in case of failure of one of the recorders.

F19.   Only good quality videotapes from a reputable manufacturer should be used. No more than one interview should be recorded on each tape. The master copy should always be recorded on a new, unused, sealed tape. Ideally the working copy should also be recorded on an unused blank tape. If previously used tapes are to be employed, any earlier recording should be erased so that the tape on which the working copy is to be made is genuinely 'blank'. The recommended maximum number of times that a tape can be erased and then recorded upon is ten. It will therefore be necessary to have a method of noting the number of times each tape is used to make a recording.

ADMISSIBILITY OF VIDEO RECORDING UNDER OTHER PROVISIONS OF THE CRIMINAL JUSTICE ACT 1988

G1.   The situation may arise where it is thought unlikely that a child will be available to go to court to be cross-examined in person. There may still be some point in interviewing the child on video[2], as it may still be possible to use a video recording in evidence even where the child does not go to court.

G2.   Under the Criminal Justice Act 1988 a statement in a document (which includes a video recording) may be put in evidence to prove any fact of which the maker of the statement could have given evidence in person. A statement made by a competent child could be put in evidence under this provision. The court would, however, require to be satisfied of certain further conditions.

G3.   First, it is not enough that the child does not want to give evidence. He or she would have to be unavailable at the time of the trial for one of the following reasons: that *he or she is dead*; or *mentally or physically unfit to give evidence*; or *outside the UK in circumstances where it is not reasonably practicable to call him or her*; or that *he or she is unable to be found even though reasonable steps have been taken to find him or her*; or that the statement was made to a police officer or a person fulfilling a similar function and *the child will not give evidence through fear or because he or she has been kept out of the way*.

G4.   Statements made by children to police officers, social workers or others who receive them in the course of their profession or occupation may also be received on the ground that the child cannot reasonably be expected to remember the facts to which the statement relates by the time of the trial. The second condition, strictly applied, is that a statement which was prepared in the course of a criminal investigation, or with a view to being used in a criminal case, will only be received under the 1988 Act if the court can be persuaded by the party proposing the evidence that it would be in the interest of justice to do so. Most video recorded interviews will be required to satisfy this second condition, which is very restrictively applied.

---

[2]Under sections 42 and 43 of the Children and Young Persons Act 1933 there is provision for written depositions from sick children to be admitted as evidence in criminal proceedings.

VIDEO RECORDED INTERVIEW

Name of child ....

Expected time, date and place of interviews(s) ....

....

I am making a video recording of my interview with
.... because I think it will spare him/her from
having to go over the same ground with my colleagues. If
there are any legal proceedings, it could be played in court to spare
him/her some of the ordeal of criminal proceedings.

If there is any information about .... you think we should know to
make the interview as comfortable as possible for him/her, please let
me know. I would be particularly interested to hear about any special
medical or dietary problems.

The video recording will be kept under lock and key and access will be
very strictly controlled, in line with the Home Office guidelines. It will
not be given to the accused although he/she will be entitled to
supervised access for legal purposes only. We will make sure we ask
permission first if it is wanted for training or any other professional
purpose.

Name of interviewer...

Contact telephone number...

SPECIMEN FORM OF RECEIPT AND UNDERTAKING

Form of undertaking recommended when receiving recorded evidence of child witnesses prepared to be admitted in evidence at criminal trials in accordance with Section 54 of the Criminal Justice Act 1991

Name of person(s) who it is proposed should have access to recording

....

Position in organisation...

Organisation ....

Address ....

....

....

....

....

Telephone ....

I/We acknowledge receipt of the recording marked "evidence of

.... "

I/We undertake that whilst the recording is in my/our possession I/we shall:

   (a)   not make or permit any other person to make a copy of the recording;

   (b)   not release the recording to [name of the accused];

   (c)   not make or permit any disclosure of the recording or its contents to any person except when in my/our opinion it is strictly necessary in the interests of the child and/or the interests of justice;

   (d)   ensure that the recording is always kept in a locked, secure container, and not left unattended in vehicles or otherwise unprotected;

   (e)   return the recording to you when I am/we are no longer professionally involved in the matter; and

   (f)   will record details of the name of any person allowed access to a recording together with details of the source of the authorisation granted to him or her.

Signed ....

for and on behalf of ....

Date ....

SPECIMEN INDEX OF VIDEO RECORDED INTERVIEW

PART I — INFORMATION ABOUT THE INTERVIEW

NAME OF CHILD ....

DATE OF BIRTH ....

NAME OF INTERVIEWER ....

POSITION ....

LOCATION OF INTERVIEW(S) ....

DATE OF INTERVIEW(S) .... NO TAPES .... TOTAL .... DURATION.................. (mins)

OTHER PERSONS PRESENT ....

POSITION ....

PART II — INFORMATION ON THE TAPE

INDEX NOS	DESCRIPTION
....	Start of the interview
....	Introductions
....	Explanation of the purpose of the interview
....	Close of interview

DETAIL OF THE OFFENCE(S)
(give child's own words where practicable and
use continuation sheets where necessary)

Child's description of the offence(s)

....	....
....	....
....	....
....	....
....	....
....	....

.... | ....
.... | ....
.... | ....
.... | ....
.... | ....
.... | ....
.... | ....

Child's description of the offender(s)

.... | ....
.... | ....
.... | ....
.... | ....
.... | ....
.... | ....
.... | ....
.... | ....
.... | ....
.... | ....
.... | ....
.... | ....
.... | ....
.... | ....
.... | ....
.... | ....
.... | ....
.... | ....
.... | ....
.... | ....
.... | ....
.... | ....

Child's information relevant to dates of offence(s)

This video-tape is the property of
[PRINT NAME AND ADDRESS OF CONSTABULARY]

It has been prepared pursuant to the
Criminal Justice Acts 1988 and 1991 and
must **NOT be copied or shown to
unauthorised persons.**

**UNAUTHORISED USE OR RETENTION MAY LEAD TO A
FINE, OR A PERIOD OF IMPRISONMENT OR BOTH**

Printed in the United Kingdom for HMSO
Dd 295784 C150 8/92 (17647)